WORK
WITHOUT
STRESS

WORK
WITHOUT
STRESS

BUILDING A RESILIENT
MINDSET FOR
LASTING SUCCESS

DEREK ROGER, PHD, AND **NICK PETRIE**

NEW YORK   CHICAGO   SAN FRANCISCO   ATHENS
LONDON   MADRID   MEXICO CITY   MILAN
NEW DELHI   SINGAPORE   SYDNEY   TORONTO

1 2 3 4 5 6 7 8 9 0   DOC   21 20 19 18 17 16

ISBN 978-1-259-64296-8
MHID   1-259-64296-8

e-ISBN 978-1-259-64297-5
e-MHID   1-259-64297-6

Design by Mauna Eichner and Lee Fukui

Challenge of Change Resilience Training™ is a trademark of Work Skills Centre Ltd.

McGraw-Hill Education books are available at special quantity discounts to use as premiums and sales promotions or for use in corporate training programs. To contact a representative, please visit the Contact Us pages at www.mhprofessional .com.

CONTENTS

ACKNOWLEDGMENTS   vii

1 A NEW WAY TO THINK ABOUT
STRESS AND RESILIENCE   1

2 WAKING UP   23

3 CONTROLLING ATTENTION   47

4 BECOMING DETACHED AND LETTING GO   75

5 DEVELOPING A RESILIENT PERSONALITY   101

6 RESILIENT COMMUNICATION AND
LEADING CHANGE   143

7 CONCLUSION: PULLING IT ALL TOGETHER   161

APPENDIX: THE RESILIENCE RESEARCH PROGRAM   169

INDEX   199

ACKNOWLEDGMENTS

We would like to express our gratitude to:

The Center for Creative Leadership, particularly Peter Scisco, for facilitating the publication of this book.

The Challenge of Change Resilience Training master trainers in the United Kingdom and New Zealand, Jo Clarke and Cynthia Johnson, for their invaluable contributions to the program over the years.

Casey Ebro and her editorial team at McGraw-Hill, for the detailed comments and suggestions on the manuscript.

WORK
WITHOUT
STRESS

1

A NEW WAY TO THINK ABOUT STRESS AND RESILIENCE

Nearly every day you'll hear people complain that they're stressed—about their job, their boss, their partner, their children. We've become conditioned to thinking that *my* stress is caused by *other* people and events, but think for a moment: can you get rid of all of these people and events from your life? You can't, and that makes stress a constant feature. You've also made yourself a victim, with your unhappiness dictated entirely by others.

This is the basic idea of managing stress: that it is a part of life that you have to learn to control and cope with. But what if this approach is a mistake? In this book we'll show you that it is indeed just a myth: stress isn't something you have to learn to live with. You can be completely free of it.

You're probably thinking you've heard all this before. Conventional stress management has been around for a long time, and it has made no difference at all. The square wheel of stress management has been reinvented endlessly, but if you look more closely, the reason it doesn't work is because it is based on fundamentally wrong principles. What is needed is not just another relaxation technique but a whole new way of defining stress: a shift in the paradigm of what we think stress is. This is not just another book about stress and how to manage it. Instead our emphasis is on *resilience*. We don't mean simply the capacity to bounce back quickly from situations we think are stressful. To be truly resilient, what's required is a shift in your mindset, so that you can see stress for what it is and choose not to become involved in it.

A new theory about stress might be interesting, but it isn't useful until the ideas have been transformed into practical strategies for actually changing our habitual ways of thinking. We will be describing a system called Challenge of Change Resilience Training,™ which I (Derek) developed from a 35-year, ongoing research program I initiated while I was at the University of York in the United Kingdom. The intellectual property of Challenge of Change Resilience Training is held by my U.K. company, the Work Skills Centre Ltd., and the training is currently delivered by accredited trainers across the United Kingdom, the United States, and New Zealand. (For more information, visit www.challengeofchange .co.uk.)

Face-to-face training provides extended opportunities for exploration and clarification, and it is undoubtedly the most effective means for acquiring skills such as resilience, but in this book we will describe in detail both the principles and practices of the system. We will provide objective, independent evidence for the efficacy of the strategies.

My research was motivated by the intriguing differences in individuals' responses to the same traumatic event: only a small proportion were subsequently shown to be suffering from stress. What was it, I wondered, that was making some people vulnerable to stress but protecting others? My research has shown that there are eight key ways of behaving that determine whether you become stressed or not, the most important of which is the tendency to *ruminate*: to continue to churn over emotional upsets.

Research is ordinarily shared with fellow scientists who have an intrinsic interest in the field. By contrast, training audiences need to be entertained, in the best sense of the word. Setting aside the skills of the trainer, the training sessions people remember most—and the ones that they're therefore most likely to practice—are those in which the content has kept them interested and intrigued to learn more throughout the process. This was our challenge. We needed to give the program a clear, cumulative sequence couched in metaphors and anecdotes that everyone could relate to. This is what we'll be describing in the book, though for the interested reader the fundamental research will be covered in more detail in the Appendix.

The research findings have been published in over 100 peer-reviewed publications and keynote conference papers, and they have been augmented by a series of case studies that offer direct tests of the effectiveness of this training. The case studies were designed using controlled-trial methodology, and they have shown significant changes in a range of performance and job satisfaction measures, including blind-assessed sickness absence. We were able to control for the extent to which participants actually practiced afterward what they'd been taught. Not surprisingly, the benefits only occurred when people used the techniques, but they were dramatic and significant. Interpreting the results of the case studies does not require detailed expertise in physiology or statistics. They are consequently far more accessible than the lab experiments, and the findings will be described at appropriate points in the book.

One of the problems we addressed when we developed the new training program was the confusion over language. For example, there is a widely held belief that there is good stress and bad stress, but since they're both called "stress," how do you know which is which? Using the terms *eustress* for the former and *distress* for the latter was just another layer of obfuscating psychobabble. From our perspective, there is no such thing as good stress. We all know how miserable it makes us, and since much of our research has involved measuring aspects of the cardiovascular and immune systems, we will be able to show you exactly how stress could significantly shorten your life. We dispensed with the psychobabble and decided to speak plainly when explaining what we meant. Later in this chapter we'll use the same plain language to distinguish between pressure and stress and between acute and chronic stress.

You may be getting the impression that by placing the onus on individuals to change, we're exonerating management practices and organizational culture, but that's not the case. Senior staff have a clear duty of care, and what that means in practice is not giving their reports anything to ruminate about. We need to learn from experience and be able to formulate effective plans, but that will happen only in the absence of rumination. Although resilience is a skill that benefits everyone, the position of control that managers have over their reports means that for them, being resilient is essential. Nick has specialized in the application of the training to leadership, and each chapter will include a section dedicated to leading change without stress. Because the steps that need to be taken to develop resilience are the same for everyone, they need not be repeated in these leadership sections, which will focus on specific strategies and consequently will have a slightly different format from the rest of the chapter.

PRESSURE AND STRESS

Do you think a bit of stress is good for you? When we put this question to our training audiences, just about everyone says yes. When we then ask, "How do you actually feel when you're stressed?" the answer is usually some form of misery, which couldn't possibly be good for you. How many people tell their loved ones what a wonderful day they had because they were so stressed? When you define it properly, stress is never good for you. In fact, all you get from it is a probably shorter and definitely more miserable life. It could never be your friend.

Stress is never good for you.

When we put these questions to people, there are always a few who say that stress energizes and motivates them, but they're not talking about stress at all. The confusion is a result of drawing a false distinction between so-called good and bad stress. Instead, we'll be distinguishing between *pressure* and *stress*. This is not just wordplay. *Pressure* is defined as a "demand to perform." The demand might be intense, but there is no stress inherent in it, and as we'll see, the key to resilience is not to turn pressure into stress.

Pressure starts from the moment you wake up in the morning, when the demand is to get up. If you doze off again, then suddenly jolt awake and realize you're now going to be late for work, pressure increases. You rush to the office, and because you were late, you're one step behind all morning. Your boss is waiting for your report, you need to reschedule the meeting you missed, and the new planning project that is on your desk needs a response by the end of the day.

Pressure + rumination = stress.

Does that sound like stress? It isn't stress at all. It's just pressure. It will become stress only if you add a critical ingredient: *rumination*, specifically *rumination about emotional upset*. If you are late, do you accept that it has happened and then get on as quickly and efficiently as you can, or are you filled with guilt about having slept in, anger at yourself for doing so, and fear of the consequences? Do you run red lights in your impatience to get to work, or swear at the driver in front who you think is slow to get going when the lights turn green? That's stress, and it serves no purpose. Traffic lights don't change for you because you're in a hurry. The driver in front doesn't go any faster, for all of your cursing. Nothing changes the fact that you slept in and now you are late. You might say that you had a critical meeting to get to, so it's no wonder you are feeling this way. Really? The problem with stress is that it will always justify itself. The simple fact is that you slept in and now you're late. Period.

You have a choice. You're not genetically programmed to ruminate.

As we'll see, rumination and how to avoid it form a cornerstone of our approach to stress. The important point here is that you have a choice. You're not genetically programmed to ruminate. It's a habit you've developed and cultivated for years. And because it is habit, it can be changed. In this book, we'll show you how. The process is very simple, just four steps:

1. Waking up

2. Controlling attention

3. Becoming detached

4. Letting go

Habits are not easy to break overnight, and it is easier said than done. Ask any smokers—they'll tell you giving up is easy; they've done it dozens of times! What you need to help motivate you is a clear reason for making the change, so we'll also show you exactly what will happen if you continue to ruminate about emotional upsets.

Although the training has been developed and enhanced over the years, the definition of stress as ruminating about emotional upset has remained the core principle around which the program is structured. People sometimes ask whether rumination is the same as worry, and it is. If worry worked, we'd run worry courses to teach people how to perfect it. A simple example: Your teenage son is out for the night. It's now 2 a.m., and he's still not home. You're concerned, but you turn concern into worry by generating imaginary catastrophic scenarios about car accidents. Yes, he might well have been in a car crash, but your worrying had nothing to do with causing it, and it would not have prevented it from happening. Catastrophic events happen from time to time, and if you've been worrying about them, your response afterward is likely to be, "I told you so!" as if you knew it would happen. If you're concerned, take action: call his friends, but avoid becoming unnecessarily stressed by catastrophizing things in your mind.

Defining stress as rumination can be difficult for people to accept, mainly because it removes the opportunity for blame. If I'm stressed because I think my manager acts unfairly, then I've exonerated myself and can justify why I'm so stressed. I'll also take every opportunity to complain about it to anyone who'll listen, which reinforces the upset and the rumination. Unfortunately, believing that stress is caused by somebody or something has become entrenched in our thinking. We talk about triggers that cause us to be stressed. But think about it for a moment: how many of these so-called triggers can you remove from your life? If you've decided they're stress triggers, you're bound to be stressed whenever they occur, and you've become a victim of your own thinking process. You complain about how stressed your job makes you, so why don't you move on? Someone sitting at the next desk probably loves doing the same job, and what this tells you is that stress is the *response* to the event, not the event itself. It isn't the trigger but *what is triggered* that's important. As you'll see, the way you respond is a habit that you can control and change.

. . . .

Stress is a response to the event, not the event itself.

. . . .

THE LIFE-EVENT MYTH

The idea of stress triggers came from the life-event model of stress, which led to the development of the familiar life-event scales. There are many of these scales around, and they typically include anywhere between 80 and 100 things that might have happened to you, like changing your job or your children leaving home. People are asked to check off all of the events that have happened to them recently, typically over the past six months. The theory behind the life-event scale is that you have a fixed capacity for coping, and since each event requires some degree of adaptation or adjustment, it will consume some of that capacity. If enough events happen, you use up the capacity and end up suffering from stress, so the more checkmarks there are on your list, the more stressed you're supposed to be. The scales later had *readjustment scores* attached to each event, which were arrived at by having a sample of people give a score to each event up to a maximum of 100 and averaging their scores for each event.

The belief that events are the cause of stress has become entrenched in our way of thinking, and hardly a week goes by without some comment in the media endorsing it. A common everyday example is moving house. In a recent radio interview, someone was describing a friend who had experienced a long catalog of changes in her life. She then added that on top of all that, this friend was moving into a new house, an event that she described as being "way up on the list." By "the list" she meant a life-event scale. If it were true that moving into a new house was inherently stressful, then everyone would be stressed by it, which is self-evidently not the case. Here's a different way of thinking: *moving into a new house is putting stuff in boxes in one place and then taking it out in another.* There's lots to organize, so there's plenty of pressure, but there's no stress unless you add rumination.

The different events on life-event scales might be interconnected: you change jobs so you also move into a new house and maybe take on a larger debt to be able to afford it, so the last two events might be an inevitable consequence of the first. The same event may also not be seen in the same way by different people.

The many life-event scales generally include items such as Christmas and divorce, and quite apart from the cultural bias in any scale that includes Christmas, the differences among people are immediately apparent. For one person, the prospect of having family around to celebrate Christmas brings joy; for another, misery! The same might be true for the partners involved in a divorce: for one, an absolute disaster; for the other, freedom at last.

To assume that events are equally stressful is plainly nonsense, even in extreme situations such as disasters, but it is important to acknowledge the effect that particular events are likely to have. For example, the event that has the highest readjustment rating on the scales is the death of someone close to you. Even if this person had been released from the suffering of a long and painful illness, it would be unnatural not to grieve, but let's put this into context: the death of someone close to you is trauma. Bereavement counseling is no different from post-trauma counseling, and the difference between everyday issues and traumatic events is that trauma can overwhelm you emotionally.

Expressing these emotions is an important part of the counseling process, and the need to do so is acknowledged in this book—as we'll see, inhibiting your feelings contributes to the impact of rumination. However, the aim of the process is to reach resolution. The length of time that may take can't be dictated, and it will vary from one person to the next, but when it is reached, the memory of the tragedy is no longer overwhelming. These two features—duration and intensity—characterize trauma. The focus of this book is on the other end of the stress continuum, what we call "everyday stress."

Inhibiting your feelings contributes to the impact of rumination.

From our perspective, events are not inherently stressful, and we needn't delve any further into the shortcomings of the life-event approach other than to highlight a comment we hear frequently: the events that make people the most stressed are the ones they can't control. The fact is that whether or not you can control things is probably distributed about 50/50—half you can control, half you can't. You should control what you can, but don't try to control what is uncontrollable because doing so is pointless. Suppose your company is downsizing and your post will be eliminated. What's the point of ruminating and getting angry and upset about it? The appropriate response is to start brushing up your résumé.

The one thing that you can exercise complete control over all the time is your attention, which we'll be talking about in Chapter 3.

RESILIENCE AND COPING

Managing stress is often coupled with coping, and a familiar model of coping is "keeping your head above water." Every now and then, the flood rises, and coping is supposedly being able to hold your breath until the flood subsides. That isn't coping. It's surviving. We offer a different perspective: that there's no water to keep your head above. Being able to see things in this way requires a change in perception, and the real challenge is not so much trying to change the world as changing your mind. There's a common phrase, "Shit happens." That's only half of what it should be: shit happens; *misery is optional.* That doesn't mean you should stay in a job you hate, feeling the flood rising the moment you walk into your office. Instead, you could ask, what has stopped you from making the move? Probably fear of imagined consequences—in other words, rumination.

Shit happens; misery is optional.

This is why this book is not about *stress management*. The term implies that stress is ever present and that it has to be controlled and managed, even supposedly made your friend. This book is about *resilience*. It is not a new concept, and it has been widely researched. It is estimated that over 100 different definitions of *resilience* have been proffered, depending on whether it is seen as an ability individuals possess, an ability to adapt to difficult circumstances, or whether there were positive changes in the individual's behavior subsequently. Unfortunately, the wealth of academic definitions hasn't resulted in greater clarity, and they all tend to presuppose that the situations people are responding to are adverse. How about the ability to see unfolding circumstances simply as ongoing change, without adding the emotional judgment of negativity to it? Resilience is not about being able to keep your head above water but realizing that there's no water to keep your head above.

Here's a scenario that illustrates what we're talking about. You're on a white-water rafting trip, and you've just come through the first set of terrifying rapids. You've rounded a bend, and the river has widened and slowed. You can hear the rush of more rapids ahead, but there's a tall cliff that prevents you from seeing around the bend. How do you feel at that moment? You don't need to have experienced it to imagine relief at being in calm water, but what else do you feel? Exhilarated and excited, but perhaps also anxious and fearful about what might be around the corner.

Resilience is the ability to negotiate the rapids of life without becoming stressed.

The river is a useful metaphor for our lives. In the river of life there are very few people who are permanently in the equivalent of rapids, and even the toughest times generally come to an end. In the same way, just as few people would say they were permanently in calm water. Life alternates between rapids and calm, so if you're in calm now, you can be sure there are rapids to come. You can't avoid the rapids, but they're not inherently stressful. What increases as you approach the next set is not stress but pressure, which, as we've said, is just a demand to perform. Pressure varies from the demand to get up in the morning to what happens when a plan goes wrong at work. Pressure can be motivating and helpful, but as the raft approaches the next rapid in our scenario, what might happen is that half the people in it start to panic. The consequence is that the raft will capsize, and you won't get through. What these people have done is to turn pressure into stress. Resilient people don't lose perspective, and *resilience* can be defined as *the ability to negotiate the rapids of life without becoming stressed.*

Here's what stress is: Imagine you have a pet cat asleep on the floor, and you walk into the room so quietly it doesn't hear you come in. At the last moment the cat wakes up, and it jumps into the air with its back arched and its hair standing on end. This response is called *fight or flight*, and it happens because of a dramatic increase in adrenaline. The next second, the cat recognizes you, and its hair flattens and it relaxes again. The outer calm that you see is because of inner calm—the excess adrenaline is quickly metabolized because it's no longer required, and the cat returns to a resting level. What your cat doesn't then do is go on thinking, "Whoa, that might have been the Alsatian from next door! What about the dogs on the other side? What if they're in the garden? If only I didn't have to live on this street!" If the cat did think like this, its hair would continue to stand on end.

Now relate the story to your own personal experience. Think back to the last time someone said or did something that really irritated or upset you. How often, and for how long did you go on thinking about it afterward? Every time you did, you provoked a fight-or-flight response, with the surge of adrenaline you saw in your pet cat. Adrenaline is not a stress hormone. It is just a hormone doing exactly what it's designed to do: facilitate action. The problem isn't the increase in adrenaline but whether or not it is needed. When you ruminate on what-ifs and if-onlys, what are you fighting or fleeing from? Just a thought in your head. After an argument that you feel you lost, you continue rerunning it in your mind, usually with you winning every time. Nothing changes: you lost, but your continuing to churn over all those imagined slights and resentments sustains the anger and upset as well as the physiological strain that comes from elevated adrenaline.

The advantage of having a clear and simple definition of stress as rumination is that it makes sense of another confusing distinction, between *acute* and *chronic* stress. Much of the evidence suggests that chronic stress is the source of the negative consequences on our health, but what's really the difference between them? We can simplify the issue by not adding stress to the acute version at all. "Acute stress" is the short-lived effect you saw in your pet cat: a temporary increase in pressure that recedes just as all pressure does. Chronic stress is what stress actually is. What makes pressure chronic? One cause might be genuine sustained demand, such as caring for a relative suffering from dementia. As we'll see when we look more closely at the physiology of stress, rumination also leads to sustained elevation in another hormone called *cortisol*, and the consequence over time is compromised immune function. There is direct experimental evidence that dementia caregivers show significantly delayed wound healing as a result of this impaired immunity.

RUMINATION VERSUS REFLECTION

In the example of the caregivers, there is no letup from the constant demand, but in practice, that's very rare. More typically, bouts of pressure are separated by opportunities for downtime, but if you go on churning about emotional upsets, the demand becomes constant. You might say that you're thinking things through to arrive at a conclusion. Thinking over a problem to arrive at a solution we'll call *reflection*, but to be able to reflect requires taking a detached perspective. This is not to suggest adopting a superficial or unengaged way of problem solving—the thinking about it might be pretty intense, but what it doesn't include is negative emotion. With reflection, what-if becomes, "What if we tried this approach? Hmm, maybe not. What else could we try?" When negative emotion is added, what-if becomes, "What if we fail? What if I lose my job? What if my family ends up on the street?" What is missing from reflection is catastrophizing.

> *Reflection is the process of thinking over a problem to arrive at a solution.*

A conventional approach to managing stress based on fundamentally misguided ideas couldn't possibly work. If events were inherently stressful, there wouldn't be anything you could do except try to escape from the events or people you're attributing stress to, and you would end up defining yourself as a victim of circumstance and using blame as a justification for your behavior. Defining stress properly as rumination shifts the source of stress to learned and hence changeable behavior, and change may well be urgently needed. Stress has a significant impact on your mental and physical health and couldn't, in any way, be good for you. Rumination allows us to define clearly what we're talking about when we distinguish between acute and chronic stress, and between pressure and stress.

We also draw a clear distinction between post-traumatic stress and everyday stress. A condition is diagnosed by identifying symptoms, and people suffering from *post-traumatic stress* show a range of changes in their behavior that can legitimately be used to make a diagnosis, such as flashbacks to the events, disturbed sleep, depression, or anxiety. These obvious changes are likely to occur only when the demand is traumatic—when it is so intense that it overwhelms the person's ability to maintain perspective. In contrast, with *everyday stress*, people can very effectively cover up how they are feeling, and there is such a wide range of potential symptoms, it would be difficult to link them to stress.

So how do you know if someone is stressed? Rather than trying to pin down specific symptoms, a useful approach is to be alert to changes in behavior, without assuming that they necessarily indicate stress. Smokers might well start smoking more than usual, but there are all sorts of other reasons why they might do so—stress is only one of them. Tiredness or a lack of enthusiasm is something most of us experience from time to time, and maybe we just need change or a break. Everyday stress is likely to be signaled by small changes such as mood swings, rather than the clinical anxiety or depression that might accompany post-traumatic stress. People generally tend to become more irritable and short-tempered when they're suffering from everyday stress, which has a lot to do with a loss of attention control. This also helps to explain why stressed people will often become more absent-minded. However, whatever you do observe, whether in yourself or in others, the important point is that the changes are likely to be maladaptive. A good example is the well-recognized tendency to drink more than usual as a way of coping. Unfortunately, if you want to deal with stress by drinking, you do need to stay drunk: when you eventually come around, things will either be the same or more likely worse! There is evidence that alcohol might have some cardiovascular benefits, and a normally functioning liver can certainly deal with modest amounts of alcohol without deleterious effects, but the only relief that drinking offers as a way of dealing with stress is temporary oblivion.

What we do know is that stress leads to a greater susceptibility to illness, but again, we need to be cautious. Conventional wisdom has it that stress causes illness and that the more stress you have, the more ill you're likely to become. The difficulty with this is that stress is in the mind when it is defined as rumination. Illness, on the other hand, is represented by measurable physical states. What's therefore being implied is that thoughts cause illness, which they do not—the impact of stress on your health is hugely overstated. Cancer, for example, is primarily a genetic disease resulting from a random mutation or a genetic predisposition. It might require exposure to a carcinogen such as tobacco smoke to trigger lung cancer, but while one person might smoke his whole life and live into his eighties, another might come down with the disease just from secondhand cigarette smoke. The latter in this example was most likely genetically predisposed; the former was not.

While stress does not cause diseases such as cancer, when the effects of genetic and environmental variables are factored out, stress still does significantly impact your health. One of the effects of habitual rumination is compromised immune function, making you more susceptible to diseases or to their spreading once you have them. What is more obvious is that stress has an enormous impact on feelings of well-being. When people become stressed, they feel miserable. Coupled with the effect it has on your physical health, the only outcome is a probably shorter and definitely more miserable life. You might have really robust genes, in which case, you may end up with a long miserable life! What is most important is that unlike genes, stress is something you can control: resilience is a skill that can be acquired through training and practice.

Defining stress as rumination might be seen as placing the burden exclusively on the individual, exonerating the role of management—"If people get stressed, they should just stop ruminating. It has nothing to do with me." Add on what that statement implies: "I'll just go on behaving however I like." Managers with this view are just that: managers, not leaders. Stress may be no more than rumination, but if you yell when people make mistakes and always blame your reports when things go wrong ("It's your problem," as opposed to "It's our problem"), you don't deserve the title of leader. You're just a manager, and a bad one at that. If you do behave like this, now's the time to change, rather than justifying your actions with comments like, "I sometimes have a nuclear explosion, but minutes later I'm my wonderful self again." Your reports suffer the fallout. Organizations do play a role, and that is to ensure that pressure isn't transformed into stress. The way to start doing that is to follow a simple principle: *don't give people anything to ruminate about.*

Singling out leaders for this example shouldn't be taken to imply that resilience is more important for them than for anyone else. Resilience at any level of an organization will improve efficiency and productivity, and the benefits are not just for work. Think back to the last argument you had with your partner, probably about something as trivial as who should tidy up the kids' mess. If you're a ruminator, you'll generate any number of angry scenarios afterward, and they'll usually generalize to all the other things your partner does that irritate you. Look more closely: they irritate you only because you'd do it differently, so in your mind your way must be better. Rumination poisons life at work and at home, and learning to become more resilient is for everyone in all situations.

However, in a work context, senior staff provide the model for how an organization operates, so we will be including examples and strategies that focus on how leaders can become more resilient.

RESILIENCE AND MINDFULNESS

To be resilient in the way we're describing means monitoring what you say and do, and that introduces another popular idea that needs to be clarified: *mindfulness.* "Being mindful" has become a buzz phrase, as "stress management" was in the 1980s, but what exactly does it mean? You might be forgiven for thinking it was invented in the last decade by psychologists, who hijacked it from an ancient Buddhist principle. It is currently used in corporate contexts to describe a technique for improving performance. The Buddha wasn't interested in improving performance. The purpose of Buddhism is enlightenment, and enlightenment is about getting who you think you are out of the way. *Mindfulness* is also used in psychotherapy, where it is aimed at making people less unhappy. The Buddha wasn't interested in happiness and unhappiness. He saw them as the same: just passing thoughts.

A different approach to using mindfulness principles is to ask the fundamental question that the word implies: what is your mind full of? If you're stressed, your mind is full of negative ruminative thoughts. You may simply be preoccupied with what you might do next weekend, and you are not ruminating about emotional upsets at all. We have a name for that: *waking sleep.* Being in waking sleep is rather like daydreaming, except that if there isn't any particular pressure on us, we might intentionally wonder what the holiday we have planned for next week will be like. A holiday daydream like this might well turn into waking sleep, when our attention becomes completely absorbed in the thoughts about it.

Like a dream at night, the thoughts become a virtual reality: a colleague asks a question, and we are literally woken up from a dream. Waking sleep doesn't cause the harm that rumination does, but the question is whether there is something else you're supposed to be doing—reviewing the report on your desk, for example. If you're in waking sleep, you're not reviewing it, and if it continues long enough, you'll be increasing the pressure to get it done when you do eventually wake up.

Waking sleep is not the same as reflection. The tendency to daydream varies from person to person, and those who do it less are bound to be more efficient, but the aim is not to be awake all the time but rather *to be more awake more of the time*. This isn't important only in a work context. How often do your friends or partner have to repeat something they've just said because you didn't hear it the first time? Waking sleep might occur because there isn't anything particular to do at the time, but it also results from boredom. Familiarity does indeed breed contempt. The key to being awake is *attention*, or rather keeping control of attention. Our attention gets snatched away, but we can learn to exercise control over it.

THE EVIDENCE BASE

We're making a lot of claims for this book, and you'd no doubt like to see some evidence. Unfortunately everyone offering training claims that it is evidence based, but on closer inspection much of what is presented as evidence is at best anecdotal. One of the main strengths of our approach is that it is genuinely based on evidence, originating in the research program Derek initiated in 1980. Research requires measuring tools, which led to the development of psychometric scales to assess the differences in personality traits that might predispose people to feeling stressed. Testing these individual differences showed that rumination was the key measure, and my research team spent the next decade running controlled laboratory experiments to establish how and why rumination was implicated in stress. The research moved away from psychology into neuroscience, emphasizing the role of rumination in the physiology and biochemistry of the stress response.

Although rumination remains the primary index, we also tested a range of other measures. These have been brought together in a questionnaire completed by training participants, called the Challenge of Change Resilience Profile, which comprises a total of eight discrete scales. Interpreting and clarifying individual profiles requires sensitivity and care, and it forms a significant proportion of the training session. For this reason the profile itself is not accessible outside of the sessions, but in Chapter 5, we will nonetheless be describing in detail the characteristic behaviors associated with each of the scales.

Our subsequent case studies showed that such behaviors as ruminating about emotional upsets can be changed. Ruminating is primarily a conditioned habit. The influence of genetics can't be discounted, and indeed, our view is that DNA is likely lurking to some degree in most of our behavior. The debate about nature versus nurture needs to be placed in the context of proportion. Eye color, for example, is genetically determined, and in a predictable way, depending on the dominance or recessiveness of the genes in question. Early resilience theories included a consideration of innate as opposed to acquired resilience, and our findings indicate that because the key component—rumination—can be changed with practice, resilience lies toward the other end of the spectrum. The aim of our book is to show you what needs to be changed and how to change it. The first step is to wake up, which is the theme of Chapter 2.

SUMMARY

- Contrary to the idea that stress is inherent in events, the key to understanding stress is to define it as *ruminating about emotional upset*.

- We distinguish between *pressure* and *stress* rather than between so-called good and bad stress. Properly defined, stress can never be good for you.

- *Acute* stress is actually pressure, not stress. *Chronic* stress is what causes damage, and apart from relatively rare circumstances of constant actual demand, what makes demand chronic is rumination.

- The research evidence that informs this book has been transformed into simple, easily understood principles, based on the need to wake up and control attention, to adopt a more detached perspective, and to let go of ruminative thoughts. If you use these principles to guide how you respond to the inevitable changes that life brings, you can be *free of stress*.

2

WAKING UP

In an average 24-hour period, how much time do you spend asleep? The answer is likely to be around 8 hours, but let's look more closely. What do you mean by "asleep"? This might sound like an obvious question, to which you'll probably answer, "Eyes closed, not aware of anything, deep and regular breathing." And what do you mean by "awake"? This also seems obvious, and the answer would probably be along the lines of, "Open my eyes, get up and dress for work, and stay that way until I go to sleep again that night." What this suggests is that there are two states of consciousness, awake and asleep.

We're not going to digress into philosophical arguments about what consciousness is, but our everyday model of a simple dichotomy between awake and asleep is oversimplified. In fact, what we hope to show you in this chapter is that people are asleep most of the time, which is why the first step in this program is waking up! The real problem, as we'll see in Chapter 3, is not just being asleep but the addition of negative emotion to the mix. Ruminating about emotional upset is what we define as stress, and avoiding rumination is the fundamental key to developing resilience. First, though, a brief overview of what we ordinarily think of as sleep.

TO SLEEP, PERCHANCE TO DREAM

Researchers draw a broad distinction between sleep that is accompanied by rapid eye movement (REM) sleep and non-REM (NREM) sleep. What happens when you drift into sleep at night is that you quite quickly move into NREM sleep, which over the next 25 minutes or so descends into a particular state called *deep sleep*. Lasting for about the next 30 minutes, your body becomes completely relaxed, and apart from essential movements such as breathing, you become very still. You're unaware of anything going on around you, you are difficult to wake up from this state, and if you are woken up, you probably feel a bit disoriented until you're fully awake.

This state of deep sleep is what we would correctly call "sleep," but during the course of the night you don't stay there. At the end of the first stage of NREM deep sleep, REM sleep begins. This is when you start dreaming, and you may move about. During this *dreaming sleep*, which lasts for about half an hour, you're easier to wake up than from deep sleep. You're not directly aware of what's happening around you or responding to it, although sounds can become incorporated into your dreams. In addition to eye movement changes, the switch between these two states of deep sleep and dreaming sleep has other characteristics that can be measured, such as brain activity. The easiest way to measure brain activity is to use an electroencephalogram (EEG), attaching electrodes to particular sites on your scalp and tracking changes in the electrical wave forms. These wave forms alter in direct response to the changing levels of sleep, with the pattern for dreaming sleep resembling that of normal waking much more than that of deep sleeping.

Do you sleepwalk, or do you know someone who does? If so, you know (or would have been told) that sleepwalkers may get up, dress for work, and even prepare food. Interestingly, it originates in NREM sleep, and it isn't necessarily an acting out of dreams. When we dream, our limbs are semiparalyzed by a brain mechanism that prevents us from acting on the dreams. In part, it seems that sleepwalkers override this mechanism, and they engage in surprisingly complicated actions. Perhaps because the brain mechanism hasn't fully matured, sleepwalking is more common in children than in adults. Because sleepwalkers engage in activities while asleep (there are claims that people have driven long distances while in a sleepwalking state), it can become a problem. It is generally regarded as a sleep disorder, and it affects as many as 1 in 10 adults.

Sleep is a complex process that isn't fully understood, and since this isn't a book about the physiology of sleep, we'll use a simple but nonetheless accurate sleep model that distinguishes between states of relative activity while asleep: deep sleep, dreaming sleep, and sleepwalking. During a night's sleep, the states might vary on a cycle of activity as shown in Figure 2.1 (sleepwalking is in parentheses because it doesn't affect everyone):

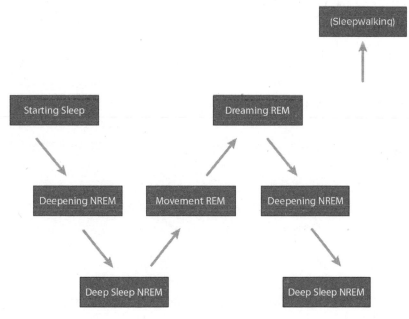

Figure 2.1

SLEEP, WAKING SLEEP, AND WAKING UP

Then the alarm rings, and you wake up, get out of bed, and start preparing for the day. But how awake are you? Are you conscious of washing, dressing, and having breakfast, or is it all happening on autopilot? All the while you may be thinking about what you need to do today, whom you may meet, and so on. You'd probably call this "planning." Dressing, making breakfast, and the rest are things you've done every day for years, so they don't require much thought, and you can focus your attention on your plans for the day. Problem is, you can become so engrossed in the plans that the toast burns and the eggs turn hard-boiled!

There is a popular idea that you can multitask, but that's a myth. The only tasks you can continue to do while thinking about other things are completely automated ones, and even then you're not actually multitasking. What's happening is that you're switching your attention from one thing to another so quickly it looks as though you're doing more than one action at the same time. So-called multitaskers are actually rapid attention-switchers. You can see how this works with breakfast preparation. Although the eggs seem to boil without your attention, every now and then, you check the timer to see how long they've been in the water, if only fleetingly, and you are hardly aware of doing so. But if you're making breakfast for a guest who eats completely different food from you that you're not used to preparing, your attention has to be focused completely on these novel tasks if you're to do them properly. You'll still be planning, but only as far as the next step in the breakfast you're making.

*So-called multitaskers are actually
rapid attention-switchers.*

What varies all the time in the process of performing tasks is the extent to which we control and give attention. Our simple breakfast example of burning the toast and inadvertently hard-boiling the eggs shows the inefficiency that results from losing control of attention—in this case, allowing it to be hijacked by thoughts about the rest of the day. We need names for these different states, so let's extend our continuum of sleep. There is *deep sleep*, which more or less refers to unconsciousness. There is *dreaming sleep*, which refers to a state in which there is mental activity but partial bodily paralysis. And there is *sleepwalking*, which refers to a state in which there are complex actions. When we're seemingly awake but have had our attention snatched away, that we call *waking sleep*. As shown in Figure 2.2, being fully awake comes only after waking sleep.

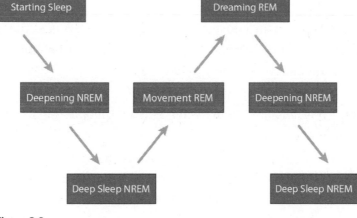

Figure 2.2

Being awake can take different forms. In emergencies, people will often behave absolutely appropriately without having had any prior experience of what they're going through, and they'll often say that everything seemed to be happening in slow motion—they had time to react to what was unfolding. The key to this state is that you're completely in the here and now, which is why we describe people who behave appropriately in emergencies as having *presence of mind*—literally, your mind (or rather your attention) is in the present. In these circumstances there's no time to think about what others have done in similar situations, and all the information you need is gained from the present moment.

Presence of mind is your mind in the present.

The reaction pattern we see in emergencies is sometimes described as the *fight-or-flight response*, but there is also a *freeze* reaction. What people say when fight or flight kicks in is that they experience no fear at all—the fear of what might have happened often only occurs afterward—but when people freeze, the emotion has caught them before they can begin to act. Derek's experience of this was being in a multistory parking garage during a major earthquake when he saw some people rigid with fear behind the wheel in their cars, completely unable to act.

Emergencies like earthquakes are quite rare, and the more common experience of being awake is when people are able to draw on remembered experience and formulate plans for action, while maintaining the present as the frame of reference. When pressure is high, this calculation needs to be done quickly, but our brains are perfectly capable of that. The sorts of situations we find ourselves in at work typically will range from high-pressure, quick decision making to deliberate thinking and planning, but the common key feature is that we're intentionally and consciously using the past and the future to make sense of the present. This purposeful planning, referring to the past and future but keeping the present as the frame of reference, we'll call *reflection*.

Waking sleep is the same as becoming engrossed in a daydream. Everyone does it, but the question is, how much time do you spend in it? Waking sleep varies from person to person, and it depends on factors such as how tired we are. Here are scenarios to illustrate waking sleep. Think back to the last time you were on the road and you reached Town X. The next thing you knew, you were in Town Y, 20 miles farther, with little or no recollection of the journey between the two towns. Or you might have gotten up in the morning and somehow arrived at work, but you did not remember getting ready and traveling the route. Perhaps you listened to the news on the car radio while waiting for the weather forecast, but five minutes later you realized that you had completely missed the forecast. During these times, between towns or between work and home, where were you?

Sometimes people say they were a blank, but you're only more or less a blank when you're in deep sleep and only definitely a blank when you're dead. Practically speaking, what you were actually doing was *thinking about the past and the future*. "What was that meeting about yesterday?" "What am I planning to do today?" "What do I need to finish that project?" "How can I engineer a meeting with so-and-so?" When these thoughts are about something in the future, we have some expectations, hopes, or fears about what might happen, which may or may not occur. To that extent, the future is fantasy. As it happens, the past is also fantasy. Bear with us while we explain.

What we call "my life" is a story we create. Everything we experience passes through the screen of our conditioned view of the world. For almost every situation, the people who experienced it will have differing versions of what happened. A simple example is the experience of people in a training program—they all heard the same presentation, but each will recall something different from what was said. Ask two people who grew up in the same family about their childhood—the versions can be so different that they might as well have been different families! The conditioned, programmed way we live much of our lives is obvious in so many simple situations. We move offices from the fifth to the seventh floor, but how often do we continue to take the elevator to the fifth floor after the move?

This is not to say events don't happen. Individuals just have different perceptions of the event because of their different associations and conditioning. What you think happened in any given situation is *your* version, usually with additions and omissions. They are, after all, just thoughts about what you think happened in the past or what might happen in the future. All of it can be described as fantasy, and if these thoughts are fantasies, then they must be dreams. And if they are dreams, you must still be asleep. You may be barreling down the road at 70 miles per hour, but you're in just another level of sleep: waking sleep.

You might wonder why there aren't many more road accidents than there are. Fortunately, there is usually a part of our attention that continues to monitor what's happening, and it responds to change. Each time something changes—a car pulling out ahead, for example—we're drawn out of the dream, and we usually respond appropriately. Unfortunately, it doesn't always work, and our engagement in the dreamworld can be so complete that we don't wake up in time. Driving while using a mobile phone is illegal for obvious reasons: your attention is on the conversation, and because you have to respond, your engagement in it can completely exclude what's happening on the road in front of you. But what about the conversation you're having in your head? That can be just as distracting. Learning to turn it off like a mobile phone is what our four steps are all about, and the first step has to be waking up.

People will quite readily recognize waking sleep in themselves, and they can acknowledge the need to wake up, but a question we're often asked is *how* do we wake ourselves up? When we sleep at night, we can set an alarm, so how do we create an internal alarm? The first reminder that needs reiterating is that waking sleep happens to everyone: nobody is awake all the time. The aim is to be more awake more of the time, and the way to create an internal alarm is to practice staying awake whenever you do wake up. If you do this, your mind will begin to develop the habit of waking up instead of going to sleep.

Be more awake more of the time.

We can start by discovering what it feels like to wake up. Wherever you might be while you're reading this, stop reading for a moment and just listen. Try to focus your attention only on the sounds you can hear now, in the moment. Notice that you'll want to classify the sound—for example, noting what kind of bird you may be hearing. This is to be expected because that's how we make sense of the world, but stop there and return to just listening. Try not to elaborate on what you are hearing into the memory of the last time you heard it, or what it reminds you of. Just listen, as closely as you can.

We often have training audiences try this exercise, asking them to listen to the sound of our voice when we're speaking, and when we're not speaking, to listen to any other sound they may hear. The atmosphere in the room changes completely, so much so that we're sometimes accused of having hypnotized everyone! We so seldom bring our minds to stillness, just registering without creating stories, that it can be quite startling. Hopefully, you've just had a taste of what it feels like to be in the present and awake. It might not last very long before the mind noise starts up again, but that's to be expected: your mind needs to be entertained, so if you don't give it something to play with, it will go off and find something. Nobody can be awake and in the present moment all the time. The key is to stay awake for as long as you can whenever you do wake up, without any self-criticism when you find you've drifted off again.

The easiest way to stay in the present is to connect with your senses. That's because your senses work only in the present: you can't see or hear anything yesterday or tomorrow. These are just thoughts about what happened or might happen. Connecting with your senses connects you with the present, and although listening tends to be easiest, the same is true for any of your senses. Remain connected as long as you can. That reinforces the habit of waking up instead of the habit of waking sleep, and you'll find yourself waking up naturally from waking sleep more and more frequently and being able to stay awake for longer each time.

Being awake doesn't require stopping what you're doing. You can connect with whatever is in the present, and that includes whatever piece of work you might have in front of you. If you don't connect with what's in front of you, then it isn't getting done. Do you get to the end of a piece of work and before beginning the next one, do you start thinking about next weekend? You may intend to do it for only 5 minutes, but it's more likely you'll wake up from the dream about next weekend 20 minutes later, by which time you're way behind schedule. Everyone does it, but there is a cost.

*The easiest way to stay in the present
is to connect with your senses.*

Here's a scenario: A report, endlessly amended, is doing the rounds and is back on your desk. You groan inwardly, but you start reading. In no time at all, you're imagining where you might go for your next vacation. The reverie is interrupted by your manager, who wants to know if you've finished with your review and reminds you that you have to present it to the rest of the team in 10 minutes. Panic! You might manage to wing it, but all this unnecessary pressure has come about because of waking sleep: you spent your attention on the next vacation instead of attending to the report. How about the last time you were in a meeting and were asked by your boss, "What do you think about this?" when in fact you were thinking of your options for lunch. Panic!

At least some of these illustrative scenarios will be familiar, if not all of them. Our mind needs to be entertained, so it will wander off if we lose interest in what we're doing. The efficiency cost involved is obvious: the more time you spend in waking sleep, the less you get done. We've acknowledged that no one is awake all the time, and repetitious tasks in particular are likely to lead to more waking sleep. We all have repetitious things to do, but the mistake is to plow on, trying to work against the growing boredom to get the job done. The result is diminishing returns and an increase in errors, which is why prolonged repetitious tasks need to be interspersed with frequent breaks to keep the mind fresh.

For almost any task you care to think of, there will be those who find it boring and others who find it interesting. That means that boring isn't an inherent quality of the job but rather something you've attributed to it. The problem is that once you decide something's boring, it will be! We tend to forget that the way we label things can make them self-fulfilling, just as saying how stressed we are all the time makes stress inevitable. Being bored with something is in part a decision you've made about it, although how quickly you become bored is in part hardwired, depending on where you are on the continuum from extravert to introvert. Extra-verts require a greater degree of stimulation than introverts, but it is important to remember that extraversion-introversion has a bell-curved distribution: most people are toward the middle of the curve. Fortunately, extraversion is not implicated in resilience. We needn't digress into a detailed discussion here, but for interested readers, a neuroscience model of extraversion/introversion can be found in the description of the research program in the Appendix.

THE NIGHTMARE: RUMINATION

We all recognize waking sleep, and we also recognize the panic that can come from being caught in our reverie. This leads to the next step after drifting into pleasurable waking sleep: the addition of *negative emotion*. After the meeting, are you preoccupied with what the rest of the team thinks about you? Do you continue to elaborate on the theme, worrying about what your boss might think, eventually ending in the nightmare scenario of losing your job, not being able to pay the mortgage, and leaving your family destitute? What you've moved into is a state of *ruminating about emotional upset*.

Rumination is the constant churning over of what-ifs and if-onlys. It's what causes stress. Without rumination, there is no stress, and rumination serves no purpose at all. Far from being use-ful or good for you, the only consequence of choosing stress is a more miserable and possibly shorter life. This book is not about managing stress, as if it were inevitable. It's about resilience, and resilient people don't get stressed. We can now be more precise: re-silient people don't ruminate pointlessly about emotional upsets. Waking sleep is the idle dream, which unfortunately can be elabo-rated easily into the nightmare of rumination, but we can choose not to do it. The implications of making the choice are hugely significant, not just for individual well-being but for organizations as well. It is estimated that 15 million working days were lost to stress-related sickness absence in the United Kingdom in 2013, and sickness absence is thought to cost the U.S. economy $227 billion annually.

There are of course ill-health conditions that prevent people from working, which is *primary* sickness absence, but a significant proportion is also attributable to *secondary* absence: being well enough to return to work but deciding to take a sick day and stay at home. Sickness absence was the focus of a case study Derek conducted among serving police officers in the United Kingdom. The gold standard for assessing change as a result of interventions is a randomized controlled trial (RCT), which is the basis for testing any new medicine. Participants in the trial are all patients with the same illness, and they're randomly allocated to either an *experimental group* that receives the drug or a *control group* that receives an ineffective substance made into tablets or capsules that look identical to the drug (the *placebo*). The patients are assigned randomly to one or the other group, and the key to who receives the drug and who receives the placebo is held in a computer file until after the study has been completed. Neither the patients nor the people administering the tablets know who receives what, which is why trials like this are called *double-blind*. At follow-up the patients are assessed to see whether there has been any change. The key is revealed only at this stage, and if the patients who actually received the drug show significant improvement in their condition compared to the controls, you can be confident that the drug has an effect on the condition.

It is difficult to create genuinely blind experimental and control conditions for training interventions, but it is possible to get a close approximation to an RCT. Our police participants were allocated to experimental and control conditions using systematic randomization: although allocation was randomized, factors such as age, gender, and length of years in service were controlled for to ensure that they were equally represented in each set of groups. One reason for working with a large employer like the police force was the substantial population from which to draw the samples based on these demographic factors. Consequently, we were able to assemble total samples of over 70 participants in each condition. For the study, they were broken down into training groups averaging 10 participants each.

Another reason for working with the police was that they had been using a conventional approach to stress management for some years. It was having little effect on the outcome measures they were using, including sickness absence, but it meant that there was a training program available that the participants were scheduled to attend at some stage. Studies of training or therapy interventions will often use *waiting-list controls*—people who are going to receive the training or therapy at some time in the future but who serve as control groups while waiting. The problem is that there's no way of knowing what help or information they might receive in the meantime, and with tests of psychotherapies the problems might in any event spontaneously remit. In our study, the conventional stress management training already in place served as the *dummy training*, which the controls received at the same time and over the same period while the experimental groups received Challenge of Change Resilience Training. The study was arranged so that the two sets of groups did not have contact during the subsequent follow-up period.

The outcome measure was sickness absence, but occasions of primary or unavoidable sickness absence were excluded. Only instances of avoidable or secondary absence were used, and the participants were unaware that sickness absence was the outcome we were studying. Secondary sickness absence over the previous 11 months was assessed at baseline and again just under a year later, and the results showed significantly lower sickness absence for the experimental groups: the average absenteeism figure for participants in the experimental group that received Challenge of Change Resilience Training was 5.39 days over the initial 11-month follow-up period, while the average for the control group that received the dummy training was 10.96 days. The results are shown in the graph in Figure 2.3.

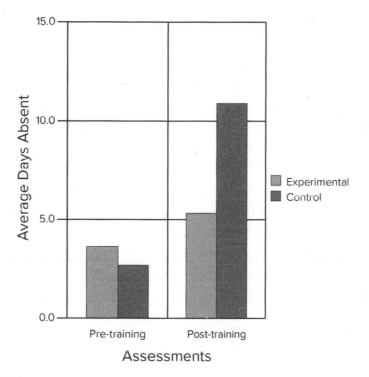

Figure 2.3

The graph shows that the sickness-absence rates increased for both groups, but this was a consequence of the 11-month inter-test interval spanning the winter months, when the incidence of seasonal minor illnesses that can compound secondary absence, such as common colds, showed a general overall increase. Controlling for seasonal effects, the control groups had significantly more days off than the experimentals, and the lower sickness-absence rate for the experimental groups was maintained through to an extended 18-month follow-up. Over the follow-up period the sickness-absence figures for the experimentals did increase slightly, but a booster session provided for a subsample from this group showed that it had the effect of reinstating the lower level of absence.

Controlling for seasonal effects, the control groups had significantly more days off.

The case study of sickness absence among U.K. police officers was the first one that we conducted. The results were replicated in subsequent studies, such as an analysis of sickness absence among managers in a large nonprofit U.K. organization providing help for people with a range of mental and physical disabilities. For practical reasons, unlike the first study, it was impossible to create a control group, but comparisons were made between the sample of managers who received the training with the average data for the other managers in the organization. Comparing the sickness-absence rates for the trained and untrained managers for the six-month follow-up period of the study with the corresponding six-month period the previous year showed that sickness absence was reduced at follow-up by between 16 and 43 percent across the four sectors, compared with a change of just 0.25 percent for the organization as a whole.

Participants in the second case study were all managers in the organization. While developing resilience is a key skill for everyone, it can have even greater implications for organizations if their leaders are not resilient, so let's consider what happens when the leaders of your organization are asleep most of the time.

WHAT ARE THE IMPLICATIONS OF LEADERS BEING ASLEEP?

Changing any behavior begins with awareness that it's happening, so for leaders to be more present and awake with their teams, they first need to notice just how much of the time *they* are spending in a dream state, perhaps while speaking with their direct reports, sitting in a meeting, or listening to a conference call. Effective leaders we meet are seldom in a dream state—they tend to be much more awake, in the moment, and paying attention to their environment, their people, and the impact of their behaviors. In other words, they've learned how to wake up and stay awake more of the time.

What do more wakeful leaders look like? Comparing the waking-sleep behavior of resilient and effective leaders with that of less resilient ones, the contrast looks like this:

Skilled in Resilience

- Spend much of their time in the present moment, fully connected with the people they are talking to rather than daydreaming about something else

- Find the present moment interesting and are curious about what's in front of them

- Realize that stories they have about the past may just be their personal version and that future plans are only possibilities

- Can quiet their minds, even amid the noise of the workplace

- See themselves as multidimensional, not defined by just one life area such as their career

- Focus on the things that they and their team can control or have influence over

Unskilled in Resilience

- Drift off into unrelated thoughts when others are talking to them and look disengaged in meetings

- Unaware of just how much time they spend daydreaming during the day

- Think so much about the future that they miss opportunities in front of them right now

- Fail to pick up on the body language of others and how they are feeling

- Focus mainly on outcomes, rather than the inputs that produce the outcomes

- Define themselves by their job: "If my work is criticized, it is a critique of me."

Describing the problem is the easy part. The question is, what can you as a leader do to develop your resilience? Here are five strategies for leaders to reduce rumination, both for yourself and for your team.

1. Connect with your senses. The fastest way to wake up and come back to the present is to literally come to your senses: what you can hear, see, feel, taste, and smell. Try the exercise we described earlier, just for 30 seconds: listen to the sounds that are close to you and then the quieter ones in the background. Notice the weight of your feet on the floor, the temperature on your face, and the shapes and colors that are around you right now. You can do this only in the present, and when you connect fully, you're wide awake. Try doing this several times in the next few days, and notice how it changes the quality of your presence.

2. Wake up the people around you. Most workplaces are full of people wandering around on autopilot, resulting in mindless meetings, inauthentic interactions, and a lack of real progress. The most effective leaders we know don't follow along mindlessly. When they see people going through the motions in meetings, they wake them up, not in a way that would embarrass them but by asking the group provocative questions. Working with senior executive teams, one of our colleagues will often ask, "What's the conversation you should be having right now but are avoiding?" People wake up, come back into the moment with their colleagues, and the energy rises. Look for these opportunities with direct reports and colleagues, to wake them up.

3. Ask direct reports questions about *right now*. Many people in workplaces suffer over things that are *not* actually happening. I (Nick) was talking to an orthopedic surgeon once about how her patients dealt with pain. She was fascinated by the ideas about waking sleep and rumination, and she mentioned how she had changed the questions she was asking her patients. She described one man who was constantly complaining of how painful his injury would be, and every time he did this, she asked him, "And how painful is the injury right now?" Often he noted that he wasn't in any pain at that moment. The more she did it, the more he realized that while the injury was real, the suffering he was experiencing was mental rather than physical pain.

In the same way, we see many workers suffering over an organizational change by imagining the worst possible outcomes. They're ruminating. When you see people caught up in the future like this, you can help short-circuit their thinking. The way to do it is not to dismiss their feelings but to bring the conversation to the question, "What problem are you experiencing, *right now*?" This offers something actual and practical you and they can work on directly.

4. Ask yourself, "What's the opportunity in front of me right now?" One reason many can't stay awake for very long is because they don't value what's in front of them. In one of our workshops, the CFO of a major airline told us that when his direct reports didn't get to the point right away, his mind drifted off. In his 360 review, he received feedback about his drifting off, and he felt embarrassed, but he didn't know how to change it.

By this time he had grasped the principle of waking sleep, so we asked him to start by considering what value or opportunity he was missing by falling asleep in the conversation. He laughed and acknowledged that he was missing the chance to coach, get to know, learn from, and influence them. "Are any of those of any value to a leader?" we asked. He had to admit that if he wasn't doing those things, he wondered if he was much of a leader. We asked him what he might say to himself when he drifted off next time, and the question he chose was, "What is the opportunity I have with this person right now?" Following up later, he told us that not only did his direct reports notice that he was more present with them but so did his wife and children!

5. Start doing walk-and-talk meetings. One of the features of highly rated leaders is that their people feel comfortable sharing their emotions with them, whether positive or negative. However, the downside of expressing emotions freely is that sometimes people get stuck talking about the same old problem over and over, without moving to a solution. One of the most effective ways to break your direct reports out of this pattern is to get them to stand up and go for a walk and talk. The walk and talk doesn't have to be long. In fact, it is better if it isn't; 5 to 10 minutes is ideal. Breaking people out of their physical patterns—sitting in the same chair in the same office complaining about the same things—and getting them to move can break the cognitive pattern. It is hard for people to stay stuck mentally when they keep taking another step forward physically.

If you can go outside, all the better, because it redirects people's attention from inward back out into the world. But that isn't essential; walking around the office can be equally effective. One manager we work with does her walk and talks in the stairwell! The only rule is to keep walking. It's not a stand and talk, nor a lean and talk. You want your people stepping forward. When the body moves, the mind will follow.

CASE IN POINT: BILL CLINTON AND LEADERSHIP PRESENCE

One of the things you often hear about great leaders such as Nelson Mandela or Mahatma Gandhi is that they have great presence. But what do we really mean by *presence*? We would suggest that the main reason that these leaders have presence is that they *are* present. When they meet you, their attention is not in their heads dreaming about last night's dinner or something clever they want to say in the next meeting. They are present with you right now.

One of the examples that comes up often in U.S. training is that of Bill Clinton. People say that he walks through a crowded room shaking different people's hands and when he comes to you, he looks you in the eye and you feel like . . . you are the only person in the room.

Great leaders have presence because they are present. What would people say about your presence? What would your coworkers say? What would your direct reports say? What would your family say?

Perhaps they would say, "It feels like he is giving me his complete attention." Or perhaps they would say, "It feels like he wants to look at his phone."

Reflect for a moment. What would the important people in your life say about your level of presence?

SUMMARY

- In a given 24-hour period, people are generally asleep for much of the time: either in ordinary sleep (deep sleep, dreaming sleep, or sleepwalking) or apparently awake but actually in waking sleep.

- Waking sleep is comparable to daydreaming, and like a dream at night, it seems real until you wake up from it.

- Waking sleep is commonplace, and it isn't a problem unless there's something in front of you that you're supposed to be attending to. You can't work and sleep, so the cost of waking sleep is inefficiency.

- Waking sleep is transformed into rumination when negative emotion is added—the what-ifs and if-onlys that serve no useful purpose and leave you feeling miserable. Rumination also prolongs the arousal required for attending to what is necessary. Your body will naturally return to a resting level so that it can recuperate, but rumination interferes with the process and prolongs the strain of the arousal to the point where it will compromise health.

- Waking sleep is not intentional. Our mind wanders into the past or the future. Being awake is about being in the present, which is why the easiest way to wake up is to connect with your senses—they operate only in the present. You can then intentionally draw on past experience and make plans for the future while keeping the present as the frame of reference. This is called *reflection*.

- Habitual rumination in leaders will significantly compromise a team's productivity and happiness.

- As a wakeful leader, reduce rumination by doing the following:

  ○ Connect with your senses.

  ○ Wake up the people around you.

  ○ Ask direct reports questions about *right now*.

  ○ Ask yourself, "What's the opportunity in front of me right now?"

  ○ Start doing walk-and-talk meetings.

3

CONTROLLING ATTENTION

The first step in the program is waking up, which we illustrated in Chapter 2 with the exercise of listening to sounds happening in the here and now. You can plan by imagining what might happen in the future, informing your plans by drawing on past experience. This is an intentional process that we call *reflection*, and it keeps the present as the frame of reference. (In contrast, *waking sleep* is an unintentional drifting into thoughts about the past or the future.) The exercise was aimed at bringing you back into the present, but it did in fact include the second step of *controlling attention*: you were invited to focus your attention actively and intentionally on the sounds you could hear. The two steps happen together, but they can be described as a two-stage process: until you wake up, attention isn't available to you. Attention hasn't stopped, but it has been so effectively absorbed in the dream that you're unaware of what's happening in the present. Waking up was described in detail in Chapter 2. In this chapter we will expand on the second step of controlling attention.

Attention is like the beam from a flashlight. Your brain is the flashlight. If someone calls your name, you swing the beam of attention to focus on who is calling and why. The person might have called you to look at a plane flying overhead, and you open your attention up to the sky, searching for it. Once you spot it, you focus your attention on that one point in the sky. Attention varies along a continuum, from sharply focused on one point or wide open to stimuli, but all along the continuum you control and give it intentionally.

Nothing happens without attention. A report arrives on your desk, and instead of dealing with it, you drift off into plans about next weekend. Attention hasn't stopped, but you've lost control of it. In waking sleep, all that attention creates is only dreams; the review of the report that you're supposed to be doing has stopped. Waking up and attending to the report is focusing attention on it. You may be drawing on previous experience to do the review, but this is the controlled thinking process of reflection. During reflection your attention can become completely absorbed in the review, but this is all happening intentionally. If the task is proving difficult, you might sit back and stare out of the window for a while, and your attention may drift back toward your plans for the weekend—whom you'll meet, what you'll wear, what you'll eat, and so on. There is no less attention involved, but you've allowed it to slip from your control and be drawn into waking sleep.

The waking-sleep thoughts about the weekend can be a welcome break from grappling with a difficult problem. It is also true that a solution will sometimes miraculously manifest in waking sleep, just as it might during dreaming sleep, but how many really useful solutions have come to you in these states of mind? One example was the discovery of the structure of benzene, which Friedrich Kekulé claimed occurred to him in dreams about a snake eating its tail, forming the ring structure that characterizes the benzene molecule. Such examples lead to an unwarranted notion that some of our best ideas come during waking sleep, but a closer examination will show that in fact, most creativity is 90 percent perspiration and 10 percent inspiration. Sweating it out happens in reflection, not waking sleep. Another mistaken idea about creativity is that it involves completely unique inspirations, but discovery means just that: *dis-covering*, taking the cover off what was already there. Creative people are able to see and make new connections between things or ideas that already exist.

Being aware of attention is really quite simple: as you're reading this page, be aware that you're paying attention to the text. Acknowledge that you can do anything in a mechanical, automated way, or you can be awake and aware of what you're doing. This brings you out of waking sleep, and it is also what will bring you out of stress.

RUMINATION: TURNING DREAMS INTO NIGHTMARES

In Chapter 2 we extended our continuum of ordinary sleep to waking sleep. Although there are efficiency costs in being absent in daydreams, there is no stress involved. The real costs begin when negative emotion is added, transforming the daydream of waking sleep into the nightmare of *rumination*. Defining stress as rumination provides a new way of thinking about stress, and it offers a simple method to avoid becoming stressed altogether.

Paradigm shifts occur when a new way of thinking replaces a previously held convention. In science, this doesn't mean that the original paradigm is rejected entirely. Einstein's relativistic physics didn't reject all of Newton's laws. Science is a cumulative process, in which a pathway to understanding is established and followed until the path takes a turn to include new information, which in contemporary science is often brought about by more advanced instruments. The turns can be very sharp, but paradigm shifts are seldom catastrophic. They can take time, especially if the new ideas are strongly resisted. People continued to believe that the earth was flat and that it was the center of the universe for a long time after those views were shown to be false. So, too, with the ideas about stress that have become so ingrained in popular thinking. For the past three decades we've been arguing that a shift in the stress paradigm is long overdue and that the conventional methods of stress management couldn't possibly have any real benefit. In this chapter we want to discuss the central, most important part of our approach, which is to define stress as nothing more or less than *ruminating about emotional upset.*

. . . .

Stress is nothing more or less than ruminating about emotional upset.

. . . .

The flat-earth view of stress is that it is caused by events and that it can in some way be good for you. Our view is that events simply offer something for you to ruminate about, but whether or not you do so is a choice that you can make. To understand this, we made an important distinction in Chapter 1 between *pressure* and stress. The conventional approach is to distinguish between supposedly good and bad stress, but in this chapter we want to show you that there is nothing useful about stress at all. Pressure, on the other hand, may be very useful, acting to motivate and spur us on, but pressure is just a demand to perform. Pressure varies, from the simple demand to get up when our alarm goes off to having to deliver work by tight deadlines. The pressure might be intense, but there is no stress inherent in it until rumination is added.

For example, at the end of a team meeting while everyone's packing up, your manager tells you across the table that you need to get a grip or soon there won't be a place for you in the organization. What happens next isn't an idle reverie about the weekend, but thoughts filled with intense emotions: anger at your manager for telling you off publicly, embarrassment in front of your colleagues, fear of losing your job. Dwelling on these emotions is rumination, but let's place it in context. What your manager is doing is telling you that you need to improve your game. He or she may have acted inappropriately in not discussing this with you privately, but that could happen for all sorts of reasons, including your manager's being in a state of rumination about the team's performance. If you leave out all the imagined negative scenarios, the demand to work harder is just pressure, a demand to perform better. There is no emotion inherent in it, even if your manager has told you this in an inappropriate way. The anger you feel is what you've added to it.

Whether or not you become stressed is a choice you can make.

We're human, so when things like this happen, we will inevitably feel the emotional effects. That's natural, but what isn't natural is elaborating them into rumination. The cost is twofold: emotional and physiological. We're all familiar with the emotional aspect, and it's no fun feeling angry or embarrassed, but these feelings will pass, and the sooner, the better! They serve no purpose other than to remind you that something needs to change, and that can be done in a reflective rather than a ruminative way. As we said in Chapter 1, worry is completely pointless. Yes, be concerned that you need to do something, which might even mean brushing up your résumé, but all that ruminating about it will only prolong the misery.

So what happens to us when we ruminate? Here's a practical example. Your company is planning a restructuring, and you've been asked by your manager to look at the makeup of your team and provide feedback on how the team might be reorganized to fit within the proposed new structure. Coming to grips with the restructuring issue may involve walking down the hall to talk to a colleague about it. You might intentionally think about the past to remember what you did the last time and whether or not it worked, as well as about the future to consider how other approaches might work. All of this is an intentional, controlled use of attention. Once the issue has been appraised, attention is then focused on the strategies to address it. When attention is given to a problem, solving it begins to progress, with new information to be processed and assimilated. In practice it is unlikely to be so clear-cut, but in principle this is a model of how work gets done. The process followed here is what we've described as *reflection*. In this scenario, it would be a case of the manager describing the proposed restructuring and the anticipated outcomes, and then you getting on with it.

Let's discuss a second scenario. This time you think, "Not all *that* again! We've just been through a restructuring that made absolutely no difference at all!" Your attention drifts away to something that seems more interesting, like the dinner you'll have with friends after work or the trip you're planning for next month. There's still attention, but now it's distracted by a daydream about pleasanter things—in other words, *waking sleep*. Since you can't work and sleep at the same time, the job you've been asked to do comes to a standstill, and it will remain that way until you wake up and return to the present. There is a performance cost but no stress. To bring stress into the picture, we need to add an ingredient: negative emotion.

Here's a third scenario. This time your manager gives a blunt overview of the issue, and on the way out he turns back and says, "Just do a better job of it this time, not like the last restructuring you messed up!" What follows is no idle fantasy about next weekend, but anger, fear, resentment, and thoughts of revenge. It's not a happy place to be.

FIGHT OR FLIGHT AND STRESS

To understand the biochemistry of stress we need to take into account three key components, the first of which is a segment of brain tissue at the base of the brain called the *hypothalamus*. This is connected by a short stalk to the second component, the *pituitary gland*. These two are connected in turn to the third component, the *adrenal glands*, of which there are two, one on top of each kidney in the small of your back (each adrenal gland has an outer part called the *cortex* and an inner part called the *medulla*). The three components act in concert, and the system is referred to collectively as the *hypothalamic-pituitary-adrenal axis*, which we can fortunately abbreviate to HPA.

A way to illustrate the connection between the hypothalamus, pituitary gland, and adrenal glands is to remember the last time you were suddenly startled—for example, perhaps you were engrossed in something in a quiet room, and a gust of wind suddenly slammed the door shut just behind you. If you had checked your body at that time, your heart would have been racing, and your hair might have been standing on end. This we've described earlier as the *fight-or-flight response*. Fight or flight doesn't just happen. It is a decision: we respond differently to different situations. We ordinarily think about decisions as rather long-winded processes of mulling over the options, but decisions can happen without all of the cogitating when they need to be made very quickly. When you perceive that whatever has happened might be a threat, your hypothalamus is stimulated, and that in turn stimulates the medulla of your adrenal gland. This is a direct neural connection, and it is consequently extremely rapid. What the adrenal medulla secretes is *adrenaline*, and adrenaline prepares you for action, increasing your heart rate and blood pressure to maximize oxygen for your muscles so that you can fight or flee.

This is *not* stress. Adrenaline is sometimes called a *stress hormone*, but it is in fact simply a hormone doing exactly what it is designed to do: prepare you for action. There is always adrenaline in your system, and it is produced elsewhere in your body, but the medulla is specialized to release a large quantity very rapidly. Adrenaline regulates arousal, and the response varies according to demand (remember, it is a decision). You might remember drifting off a bit during a talk or a meeting, and then someone said something that really interested you. Ping! You suddenly became alert, facilitated by an increase in adrenaline, albeit a much smaller response than the crash of a door slamming unexpectedly behind you.

With a full-blown fight-or-flight response, adrenaline levels rise dramatically, so much so that you can really feel the effects of an adrenaline rush, though you can't become addicted to it. So-called adrenaline addiction is simply a desire for stimulation regulated by the same physiological process. Fight or flight is also accompanied by an increase in the secretion of *endorphins*—that is, naturally produced morphinelike hormones that help to reduce the perception of pain. Endorphins are probably responsible for soldiers being unaware of wounds they've sustained. The link to morphine led to muddled notions about athletes who push themselves to their limits being addicted to endorphins. There is no such thing.

In some respects fight or flight doesn't entirely capture the way that people respond to intense demand. We've also described *freezing*, when the emotion catches you and leaves you literally frozen by fear. *Fight or flight* describes an entirely appropriate response. Although some animals freeze to merge into the background and escape by becoming invisible to predators, freezing or panicking are likely to lead to disastrous outcomes. We saw that with our white-water rafting metaphor in Chapter 1, and with Derek's actual experiences during a major earthquake. The complex emotional responses we make are mediated by the interactions with other parts of the brain, but whether you react by fighting, fleeing, freezing, or panicking, all of it is associated with a dramatic rise in adrenaline.

The increased physiological arousal provoked by adrenaline is not stress per se, but there is a significant potential cost involved. Imagine a river with a bend in it. The flow of water will cause an increase in the pressure against the outer bank of the river as it turns the bend. When the river floods during a storm, the pressure increases to the point where that outer bank begins to erode and collapse. Now substitute for the river your coronary artery, which emerges from the top of your heart and loops back down to feed the heart muscle itself, with many bends and forks. The increase in adrenaline is equivalent to the flood. The rise in blood pressure and heart rate means an increase in cardiovascular strain, and like the outer bank there may be damage to a fine layer of cells that lines the inside wall of the artery. The purpose of this layer is to help inhibit the accumulation of blood-borne fat sticking to the wall of the artery, which can happen if there is a lesion or damage to the cell layer. The fatty plaque that forms can harden and eventually block the artery, resulting in a form of heart disease called *athero-sclerosis*. Sustained high levels of adrenaline are linked to chronic high blood pressure.

How does all this relate to stress? Think about the last time someone said or did something that really annoyed or offended you: how often and for how long did you go on thinking about it afterward? Every time you did, you provoked fight or flight. It may not be as intense as when the event happened, but it increases and is sustained for as long as you are thinking about it. This is ruminating about emotional upset. Most of us know that cows are ruminants: they bring up the cud, chew for a while, swallow it, and then repeat the process. At least this is useful, gradually breaking down the cellulose in the grass so that it can be digested. Churning over emotional upset serves no purpose at all, except to make you miserable and potentially to shorten your life.

People sometimes say that it's human nature to ruminate. That suggests that it is natural, but doing something that makes you miserable and might shorten your life couldn't possibly be natural. Nature is a self-regulating system devoted to preserving the species, so what's natural is not ruminating. Rumination is also defended with the claim that you learn from doing it, but all that you're learning is how to self-inflict misery. Thinking that you learn from rumination is confusing rumination with reflection. The distinction between them can't be overemphasized. Reflection is problem solving (thinking through things without becoming involved in emotional upset), and it requires taking the third step in the program, *becoming detached*. Ruminating is churning over an imagined sequence of what-ifs and if-onlys repeatedly, and it solves nothing. To paraphrase Mark Twain, some of the worst things in your life never happened.

Defining stress in this way allows us to remove it from the event and to focus not on the triggers but on what is triggered: a cognitive-emotional response, interpreting what has happened and responding emotionally to it, coupled with the physiological changes that facilitate action. As we've said, this isn't stress, provided that we can return to a resting level as quickly as is practicable. If rumination is triggered, the reaction is extended beyond what is useful. Resilient people don't ruminate, which is why they're able to adapt so effectively. Think about it as equivalent to a motor that's run flat out continuously, compared with a motor that's run on full only when it's needed. Our bodies are designed to do the latter. Rumination overrides this natural tendency toward *homeostasis*, which is returning quickly to rest and recuperating from any wear and tear of the cardiovascular system.

Resilient people don't ruminate.

Hormones such as adrenaline serve to translate perceptions into actions, and the process is entirely appropriate if the demand is not perpetuated by rumination. Another hormone that has a known effect is *cortisol*, which, like adrenaline, is erroneously described as a stress hormone. Cortisol is secreted by the outer part of your adrenal gland, the cortex, but the response is slower because where adrenaline is provoked by an extremely rapid nerve signal, the trigger for cortisol is hormonal and acts via the bloodstream. Cortisol also involves the HPA axis, but we need to add a further detail: the hypothalamus has a front (*anterior*) and a rear (*posterior*) segment, and it is the posterior segment that directly stimulates the adrenal medulla to secrete adrenaline. The anterior hypothalamus secretes a hormonal stimulant, called a *releasing factor*, into a duct that is connected to the pituitary gland. The releasing factor stimulates the pituitary to secrete adrenocorticotropic hormone (ACTH) into the blood stream. ACTH is attracted to the outer part of the adrenal gland, the cortex.

When ACTH reaches the cortex, it provokes it to secrete cortisol. Cortisol has a range of functions, one of which is that it acts as an anti-inflammatory (the synthetic drug *cortisone* is based on the cortisol molecule). Inflammation is an entirely appropriate tissue-based response that occurs at the site of any injury sustained in fight or flight, but runaway inflammation can inhibit blood circulation to the affected area and retard healing. Another function of cortisol is to regulate energy levels by facilitating the release of stored sugar (*glycogen*), which provides the energy to fight or flee. It also conserves energy to deal with the immediate demand, and it does so in part by temporarily suspending high-energy processes such as producing certain types of white blood cells. There are several different specialized white blood cells, but cortisol has been shown to reduce both *natural killer* (NK) *cells* and to compromise *T cells*. NK cells are the frontline defense, acting quickly against a range of pathogens, while T cells regulate the overall immune response.

Continuing to churn over emotional upset maintains elevated levels of both adrenaline and cortisol. This helps clarify the difference between acute and chronic stress that we described in Chapter 1. Most of the negative effects of stress come from chronic rather than acute stress. When there's an intense demand, such as having to complete a job by a deadline, you'll feel the pressure, and your blood pressure and heart rate will rise as adrenaline levels increase to meet the demand. There are very few people who are under constant pressure like this, 24/7, so there are always opportunities for the emotional effects to recede so your body can recuperate. What makes the pressure constant is continuing to ruminate about the emotional upset in the absence of anything actually happening. Rumination *is* chronic stress. Acute stress isn't stress at all, just pressure. The physiological effects we've described are well established, which is why stress can never be good for you.

STRESS AND EMOTION

Fight or flight is not just a physiological response. What triggers and sustains it is emotion. Although we've defined stress in terms of emotional upset, there's nothing wrong with emotion. Emotion is part of what makes us human, and almost everything we do involves emotion. For example, different aspects of your job can be ranged along an emotional continuum, from "I hate doing this" to "I love doing that." If you have an inbox, the bottom will be filled with "I hates." Unfortunately, they don't just disappear, and you find your attention repeatedly being distracted by remembering that they're still there. One day you decide to do only them, and you then wonder what the fuss was all about! The fuss was put there by your not wanting to do the jobs and preferring to do something else, which was an emotional prioritization rather than a rational one.

Instead of prioritizing according to what's most important, try doing the reverse: begin by deciding what isn't important and needs to be trashed. Managers often impose on their reports the completely unrealistic expectation that they should do everything they are sent. When did you last get everything done? I recall a training session in which a manager turned to his team halfway through and said he didn't expect them to do everything he gave them. A refreshingly enlightened view, though he did include an important rider: that the important things needed to be done 100 percent. If the team tried to do everything, they'd be lucky to deliver 70 percent, so prioritizing needs to be a continuous process that begins with identifying what isn't important.

To make this decision requires keeping in perspective the emotion that clouds our judgment and turns prioritizing into preferring, but there may be a real problem in deciding what to focus on. Your manager has given you three tasks to attend to, but you realistically have time to complete only two of them satisfactorily. Which are the most important? The way out of that dilemma is consultation—that is, asking your manager directly. If she is a leader, she will be able to see that her expectation wasn't realistic, and she will make recommendations: "Focus on these two, and if the third doesn't get done, we'll make another plan." A mere manager (rather than a leader) will simply tell you to make sure you deliver everything. Changing jobs in tough economic times is neither simple nor easy, but it may be time to brush up the résumé—managers who disregard the constraints of time and money and make unrealistic demands are not worth reporting to.

In fact, with fewer workers doing more, the inevitable consequence is that everyone has too much to do. You can learn to manage the time available more effectively, but there is no training program that can create more of it. The conventional wisdom is that you need to work smarter, but no one tells you how to do it—don't you just end up pedaling faster? It is possible to work a lot smarter, but the key to doing so is to be more awake.

Although emotion is an inevitable part of how we respond, it does need to be kept in perspective. The danger with emotion is not that it occurs but rather that there is potential for you to become involved and overwhelmed by it. The key to resilience is to avoid turning pressure into stress by needlessly adding in negative emotion and feeding it with attention. People sometimes say that without stress, they wouldn't be sufficiently motivated, but what should motivate us is passion for the work, not stress. Stressed people work less well; all that the myth about stress being good for you has done is to provide bad managers with a justification for making impossible demands.

* *

It is possible to work a lot smarter, but the key to doing so is to be more awake.

* *

Emotions won't stop when you become more resilient, but what does become available is a choice about how you continue to respond. The most important choice is not to ruminate about the emotional upsets, but there is another choice included in our model, which is whether or not you express your emotions. Derek's research program was aimed at identifying the personal factors that made people more vulnerable to stress, and in addition to the key measure of rumination was a scale for *emotional inhibition*. These two measures formed part of what was called the Emotion Control Questionnaire (ECQ), and studies using the scales showed both that stress *is* rumination and that its effects can be mitigated by expressing rather than inhibiting emotion.

Rumination was unique to the research program, and the ECQ represented the first published index of rumination, but it wasn't a great surprise to find emotional inhibition emerging as a factor as well. The benefits of saying how you feel is expressed in common aphorisms such as "A problem shared is a problem halved," and much of the research at the time had shown the importance of this aspect of emotional response style. Getting things off your chest is the feeling of pressure being released.

The reasons people bottle up or inhibit emotion are many and varied, but central to it is the idea that expressing emotion is a sign of weakness, and doing so will make you vulnerable. In fact, the opposite is true. In the same way as not ruminating, expressing how you feel is a sign of emotional intelligence. It was also not too surprising to find a significant gender bias, with women far more willing to share their emotions. There can be little doubt about the greater emotional intelligence of women, who know and understand their emotions; for many men, how they feel is an embarrassment best kept secret. We do need to be clear, though, that we're talking about the *appropriate* expression of emotion. We're not advocating indiscriminate disclosure! People who are always venting have often just developed the habit of doing so. They're not getting any resolution, and there are no benefits in it for them or the people who have to listen to it all the time.

Expressing how you feel is a sign of emotional intelligence.

The appropriate expression of emotion means not becoming identified with the issues all over again but, rather, talking about them in a way that leads to putting them in perspective. It is equally important that the listener maintain perspective and avoid becoming identified with the discloser's issues. This is what *empathy* is. Becoming identified with others' issues leads to *sympathy*, and nobody is helped by sympathy—you just have two people with the problem instead of one. Empathy is a cornerstone of effective leadership.

TAKING THE FIRST STEPS

When it comes to waking up, unfortunately, there is no magic bullet. The training program is not the road to Damascus, and like any useful behavior, it requires repeated practice if it is to become a habitual response. The first step of waking up can become habitual surprisingly quickly. In our training program, the sessions are sometimes split into two periods, with time in between for reflection and practice. The gap need only be overnight, and the homework is to ask participants to notice how much time they spend in waking sleep. On their return for the second period, everyone has become aware of periods of waking sleep. It isn't that waking sleep has suddenly started or has increased but, rather, that people have become aware that it is happening. It is also typical that some return to the second period extremely concerned to have discovered just how much time they spend in a dreamworld, but they can easily be reassured by asking them how they knew they were in waking sleep. The answer has to be because they'd already woken up—knowing about waking sleep is always retrospective. Waking sleep is, after all, another level of sleep, and just as you wake up from a nightmare and realize it was only a dream, you know you were in waking sleep only after you've already woken up.

Having woken up, attention then becomes available to be used and directed intentionally to the tasks at hand. People sometimes say that what makes them feel stressed is not being in control, but they're often talking about things that they have no control over anyway. The one thing you always have control over in principle is your attention, and that's what really needs to be controlled. Something else many commonly say is that they do wake up, but it is all too easy to slip back into waking sleep. This is exactly what people find when they start to practice. Remember, nobody is awake all the time. The aim is to be more awake more of the time. A useful motivation to being more awake is to recognize the efficiency costs of waking sleep.

Realizing the significant health costs of rumination can certainly help to focus the mind, but it also helps to remember that rumination is a habit that can be changed. Our case studies have provided direct evidence for that. For example, in a large New Zealand company, we included staff from two sectors of the organization that were located in separate buildings. Challenge of Change Resilience Training had been planned for groups from both sectors, but while the groups from one sector received the training, it had to be postponed for the other sector. This provided the opportunity to compare experimental (trained) and control (untrained) sets of groups. In preparation for the training, participants from both sectors had completed the Challenge of Change Resilience Profile, which includes a measure of rumination (the profile comprises eight different dimensions, which we'll be describing in detail in Chapter 5). One of the shortcomings of readministering tests is that participants' responses are biased by recall, which was minimized by using a 13-month interval between testing.

The readministration of the profile showed a significant decrease in rumination scores for the trained group, while scores for the untrained group were unchanged. Because of continuing work with the company, it was possible to interview participants at the second administration of the tests to determine how much they had practiced the principles they had learned in the training program. The measure was an informal one, but nonetheless the trends indicated clearly that change had occurred mainly among those who had continued to practice the principles of the training. This is hardly surprising—training offers little benefit unless it is subsequently put into practice, but it was helpful to be able to confirm the effect.

Training offers little benefit unless it is subsequently put into practice.

Further evidence for change as a result of the training came from analyzing the results of a climate survey that Derek developed as part of his work. The Challenge of Change Resilience Training Climate Survey was constructed using the same rigorous psychometric procedures that the profile scales were based on, generating items by asking respondents from a wide variety of employment sectors and levels to reflect on their experience of work, current and previous, and to say which positive features made organizations great to work for and which made them negative workplaces. The preliminary questionnaire based on their responses was given to a large sample of working people, again from a wide range of sectors and levels (gender was balanced), who were asked to rate their current organization on each item using the 4-point scale. Their responses were subjected to exploratory analysis to decide a final form of the scale, which was endorsed by subsequent confirmatory analyses.

The analysis yielded four workplace factors or components that are labeled Management Style, Empowerment, Workload, and Communication. The labels for the factors are to some extent self-explanatory. The first dimension reflects general perceptions of the overall management style in the company, the second the degree to which people feel they are able to act independently, the third the perception of how heavy the individual workload is, and the fourth the perception of how open and effective the communication of information is in the company.

Using the statistical weights for each item, the four dimensions were regularized to comprise 10 questions each, which means that scores range from zero to 30; scores in the range from 20 to 30 represent positive perceptions of organizational climate. Of the four dimensions, average scores for Workload tend to be lower than the other three, reflecting the relatively increasing workload that has generally been experienced in most economies in recent decades.

The four dimensions do correlate fairly strongly and can be pooled to provide an overall measure of organizational climate, but using them independently offers a more targeted and detailed picture of employees' perceptions.

The readministration of the climate survey in the second case study provided before- and after-training scores for the groups that received the training, as well as first and second administration scores for the untrained groups over the same period. The results showed a significant increase or improvement in scores for the trained groups on three of the dimensions (Management Style, Empowerment, and Communication), as shown in the graph in Figure 3.1.

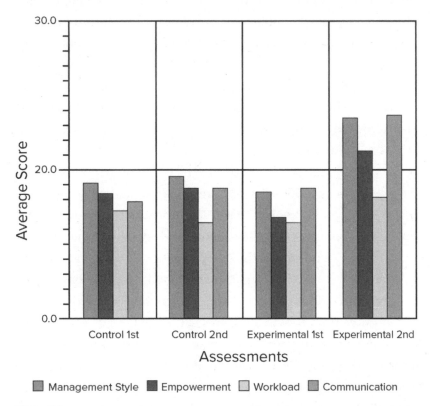

Figure 3.1

The lack of significant change in the Workload factor of the scale was not surprising. Workload is in fact a measure of pressure or demand, and neither this training nor any other will reduce pressure. Together with the findings for the rumination dimension, what the results revealed was the same degree of pressure but a less stressed (in other words, less ruminative) way of responding to the pressure among those who had received the training.

STRESSLESS LEADERSHIP

There is no question that leaders in the twenty-first-century workplace are under increasing pressure. Each year we work with over a thousand leaders in our training programs whose workplaces are characterized by BOCA conditions:

- **Blurred boundaries** where new technologies mean that work has penetrated all times and locations

- **Overload** from the volume of work exceeding the ability to keep pace with it

- **Complexity** of problems becoming more systemic and difficult to solve

- **Addictive**, meaning that many leaders with high-achieving personalities are addicted to the stimulation of work

And that's just at work. Much of what people describe as workplace stress is actually stress they carry from their personal lives: ruminative thinking isn't something you leave at the door to your office. The opposite is equally true: rumination won't necessarily stop when you walk through your front door. Minds are portable, and we carry our thoughts with us wherever we go. What might change is the *theme* of the rumination: when we ask participants in our workshops to list their pressures at work and at home, the top three for the former are workload, change, and deadlines, and for the latter, family, health, and finances.

With all these pressures, is it possible to lead yourself and your team and be happy at work and at home, without getting completely stressed out? The answer, as proven by many of the leaders we work with, is a definite yes. We describe those who don't get stressed—in other words, who don't ruminate—as being resilient, but we've also emphasized that rumination is a habit. It may be a well-practiced one, but habits can be changed, so resilience is a skill that can be acquired by training. It all begins with waking up, and leaders who often drift off into waking sleep are constantly saying how stressed they are. They lack resilience skills. Comparing their habitual behavior with the skills of resilient and effective leaders, the contrast looks like this:

Skilled in Resilience

- Understand the difference between pressure (external demand) and stress (rumination), and teach their people to do the same

- Accept that pressure is a natural part of having a job, whereas stress is chosen

- Focus on what they and their team can control or have influence over, especially their attention

Unskilled in Resilience

- Constantly think about the what-ifs and if-onlys, without realizing they're ruminating

- Imagine events to be bigger and more consequential than they really are

- Ruminate about other people and what others might think of them

We've said many times that resilience is a learnable skill, so here are four practical steps leaders can take to enhance their resilience.

1. Help your team differentiate between pressure and stress. Most people think these two are one and the same. They are not. Don't you know some people who face very little pressure in their lives but are very stressed? Don't you also know some people who face a great deal of pressure and yet are not stressed at all? In our workshops we often ask, "Does everyone in this room face pressure?" Everyone nods in agreement. Then we ask, "Is everyone in this room stressed?" There's usually a silence before someone says, "Yes, of course we're all stressed," but others then speak up: "No, I'm not stressed." When scores from the profile are discussed in the group, the leaders realize that everyone in the room is facing roughly the same pressure but that the stress levels vary widely.

While it is not a universal rule, we often see in our work that the higher people go in the organization, the less stressed they are. You might argue that this is because people at the top have it easier. That could be true, but we doubt it. Looked at more closely, the truth is that those who keep getting promoted are most often the ones who can handle more and more pressure without turning it into stress.

2. When you wake up from ruminating, ask the question, "How useful was that?" When I (Nick) first learned about Challenge of Change Resilience Training, I was going through a high-pressure health challenge, and I realized I was ruminating constantly. One exercise that helped enormously was to ask myself, "How useful were the last 12 minutes of rumination?" It was a genuine question because I felt that perhaps some real value had been created by doing it. I discovered that no matter how many times I asked, there was never an occasion when anything useful came of it. This contradicts the belief that many ruminators have, that rumination needs to be maintained because it has some useful purpose. Once you start to see that your ruminations serve no purpose, the grip that these pointless, negative thoughts have over you starts to release.

3. Scratch the rumination record. Many still remember what it was like to play records on a turntable. A new record would play perfectly, but as it got older and scratched, the needle would start to jump out of the grooves. If you scratched the record enough, pretty soon you couldn't play those familiar tunes at all.

Rumination is like a record. We have favorites that we play over and over in our head without any helpful outcome ("Does my boss hate me?" "What if there are layoffs?"). What we need to do is scratch the record as soon as it starts playing. We do this by interrupting our thoughts as quickly and powerfully as we can. Once you've taken the vital first step of waking up, one of the most powerful ways to maintain this state is to physically move: stand up and go for a brisk five-minute walk. Don't fall into the trap of spending the entire walk continuing with the rumination. Connect with the present for as much of it as you can. The way to do that is to remain connected to your senses. When you move with intention, you get out of your mind and back into your body and the world around you.

4. Turn rumination into reflection. Some leaders are confused by the distinction between rumination and reflection. Both involve thinking, but they couldn't be more different. Figure 3.2 shows a good way to illustrate the difference by using a simple visual representation that has a threshold shown by a horizontal line.

Above the Line	• Planning for the future and drawing on experience, but keeping the present as the frame of reference • Acknowledging that your recall of the past may not be accurate and that plans for the future are based on probability, not certainty • Ensuring that everyone is included in the decision-making process, but confident in making a final decision
The Line	
Below the Line	• Churning over the if-onlys about the past and the anxious what-ifs about the future • Insisting that events were exactly the way you remember them and having inflexible, no-plan-B expectations • Imposing your views and responding angrily when they're questioned

Figure 3.2

When you think about the past or the future in a positive or even a neutral way, this is reflection, and we call this *above-the-line thinking*. Rumination is *below-the-line thinking*. Reflection is essential for good leadership, while rumination is disastrous. When you catch yourself thinking about something, stop and ask yourself,

"Am I reflecting in a positive or neutral way, or am I ruminating and making myself stressed?" The former helps you create direction, alignment, and commitment for your team. The latter will lead to a short, miserable life. Choose wisely!

CASES IN POINT

Power Plants

We once worked with a group that included electrical power plant managers. During the first session one of the leaders asked if we were actually telling a group of *power plant operators* that they should never think about what could go wrong! The answer of course was no, we were not saying that. What we were saying was, think about it, plan for it, be ready for it—just don't fall below the line and ruminate about it.

The rest of the group then shared that, in fact, the worst person to run a power plant would be a chronic ruminator, who would make everyone anxious. In their view, the best managers were those who could look at the plant and their work in a detached way, which allowed them to do two things:

1. Plan for what could go wrong and how to respond, without ruminating about it (future focus)

2. Reflect on past mistakes so that they could learn from them (past focus)

Football Teams

We saw the same principle in action with a professional football team. On the Monday morning after each game, the players would gather in the film room, and the coach would play a video of key parts of the game. He would constantly stop the video to point out what they did well on a particular play and where they had made mistakes (learn from the past). Once they had watched the whole game, the coaches would then switch the players' focus toward the next game and what they needed to do to prepare (plan for the future). For the rest of the week the players practiced implementing that plan to the highest quality possible (focus on the present). The players and coaches didn't ruminate about the last game or the next one. They stayed above the line and used all three time dimensions—past, present, and future—to get the job done as well as they could.

SUMMARY

* Stress is rumination, which turns pressure into chronic worry and sustains fight or flight when there's nothing to fight or flee from.

* Resilient people don't ruminate.

* Resilience isn't a matter of being able to surface more quickly when you're submerged by the flood of feeling that you have too much to do. Resilient people know there's no flood to survive—just pressure that comes and goes.

* Waking sleep has efficiency costs, but the real costs come with the addition of ruminating about negative emotion. To escape from these dreams and nightmares, we need to wake up.

* The habit of going into the dreamworld is countered by staying awake for as long as you can whenever you do wake up.

Nobody is awake all the time, so waking sleep will always occur, but rumination—and therefore stress—can be avoided altogether.

- Once you're awake, attention becomes available for you to use intentionally. There is attention in waking sleep and rumination, but it's been hijacked by your thoughts.

- Expressing emotion is helpful in mitigating the effects of rumination, but it needs to be expressed appropriately.

- As a wakeful leader, you can help your teams do the following:

    - Differentiate between pressure and stress.

    - Upon waking from rumination, ask, "How helpful was that?"

    - Scratch the rumination record.

    - Turn rumination into reflection (practice above-the-line thinking).

4

BECOMING DETACHED
AND LETTING GO

Wake up and control attention: these are our first two steps in the process of freeing yourself from stress and becoming resilient. The more you practice staying awake for as long as you're able to whenever you do wake up, the more frequently it happens and the longer it lasts. Practice also shows you how easy it is to control attention once you have woken up from waking sleep, but you've probably found that the effect can be quite short-lived. The danger is in thinking that this is easier said than done and that you just can't maintain your connection with the present, and then giving up. The fact is that attention *will* drift off as your mind looks for stimulation, but it is equally true that it will become increasingly easier to wake up and connect again.

Drifting off is bound to happen more frequently with repetitious tasks that you don't enjoy doing, but you will also have experienced the ease with which attention can be controlled and held: think back to the last time you were engaged in an activity you really loved and how easy it was to stay connected. In those circumstances the potential distractions or thoughts just pass by. To be able to do this, you are in fact taking the last two steps in the program, *becoming detached* and *letting go*. All four steps are necessary: it is a four-stage process, and to be really successful, you need to follow through all four of them.

WHAT DETACHMENT REALLY MEANS

The research was aimed at finding out what it was that made people more vulnerable to stress. We've already described two factors: rumination and inhibiting emotion. Another of the psychometric scales to emerge from the research was a measure of coping, which we call *detached coping*; the third step in the program is based on this measure. Language is double-edged—words can serve either to make things as clear as crystal or as clear as mud. Part of the problem is that we each have particular associations with words, and this is certainly true with the word *detachment*. For many, this conjures up a sense of being disengaged and separate, of not caring, which is definitely not what we mean—in fact, you can really care only when you are detached. Others see a connection with the Buddhist principle of nonattachment, which is much closer to our use of the word, though a study of Buddhist teachings is not required for resilience!

Let's be precise about what we mean when we use the word detachment: *being able to maintain perspective*. Detached people don't turn molehills into mountains, while those who are not detached endlessly catastrophize and blow everything out of proportion. A lack of detachment and the tendency to ruminate are intertwined in a spiral of stress: when you ruminate, things balloon out of proportion, and when things are out of proportion, you're more likely to ruminate. This clarifies the distinction between rumination and reflection: *you can reflect only when you're detached.*

. . . .

Detachment means being able to maintain perspective.

. . . .

Detachment is a familiar idea. When something goes awry and people start to lose perspective, the detached member of the team will use a phrase to bring everyone back down to earth, maybe saying "No one has died." This is not intended to trivialize the issue. There are complex and difficult problems to solve, but catastrophizing them will certainly not lead to a solution. Other familiar phrases include "It's only a job" or "Don't sweat the small stuff," but we can go a lot further than that: Why sweat any stuff? All you get is sweaty!

The extent to which you're able to maintain perspective will of course depend on the emotional intensity involved. From time to time most teams will fail to deliver, but what about when someone close to you does die? We've said that bereavement is at the post-traumatic end of the distribution, and you may be overwhelmed by the intense emotion of bereavement and loss. It remains true that even with bereavement there are significant differences in how people respond. If you are overwhelmed by emotion, it is important not to try to suppress it. Bereavement is a consequence of intense attachment. It is emotion in varying degrees that attaches us to everything, which is why the more intense the emotion, the more difficult it is to maintain perspective.

. . . .

Why sweat any stuff? All you get is sweaty.

. . . .

However, the focus of this book is day-to-day stress, and when you're dealing with issues that are coming up all the time, maintaining as detached a perspective as possible is essential. This should not come as a surprise—most of us have experienced the difference between those times when we've lost it and those when we've been able to keep things in perspective. What we lose is control of attention—at which point, molehills grow into mountains, and we act completely inappropriately, becoming angry, fearful, or tearful. To be able to keep control and maintain perspective, we need to conclude the process by *letting go*.

LETTING GO

The simplest way to explore detachment is to link it to the fourth and final step in the program, *letting go*. We can illustrate it with a story about how to catch monkeys. You start by taking a pot with a hole in it just big enough for the monkey to squeeze its hand in. You tie the pot to the ground, put one peanut inside, and hide behind a tree. The hungry monkey puts its hand through the hole and grabs the peanut, but now its fist is too big to pull back out again. The pot's tied to the ground, so you can run up and catch the monkey. The forest is full of food, but it won't let go—it gives up its freedom for a peanut. All it had to do was to let go!

The story provides a perfect metaphor for our definition of stress. All this stuff we hold on to and ruminate about is peanuts, just what-ifs and if-onlys that are of no consequence now and never will be. The effect of rumination is a shorter and more miserable life, but like the monkey, all you need to do to be free is to let go. This is the final step in the sequence of four steps to be free from stress. Until you wake up, you remain locked in the nightmare of rumination, but once awake and back in the present, you have the opportunity to regain control of your attention, to put things in perspective, and to let go of the negative emotion with which the issue has become entangled.

All this stuff we hold on to and ruminate about is peanuts.

THE HOUSE OF THE MIND

Imagine the mind as a simple house: one large room with two doors, one at each end. Picture a flood of water on one side of the house (it is just a metaphor!), kept out by the door on that side. The flood represents everything we might think about, all of which carries an emotional charge, usually along a continuum from positive to negative. The good thoughts might be useful, such as solving problems when we reflect on them, and the emotional charge may be more neutral than specifically positive. The good thoughts might also be the pleasant distraction of waking sleep, planning your next holiday.

The way the model works is that you're only consciously aware of anything when it's inside the house, so to be aware of the thought, it has to be brought in through the door.

You could describe this as bringing something to mind, and although the memory is represented by a thought, it is in a physical part of your brain. What you're exposed to becomes part of your neural network. By retrieving the memory, you're initiating a bioelectrical process that stimulates the nerve cells that represent the thought. The relative permanence of memory is in part a function of emotion, so everyday memories are likely to disappear completely when those nerve cells are resorbed, whereas those associated with powerful emotion are more likely to endure. This is why catastrophic events we've experienced can always be recalled, and it's why you can remember exactly what you were doing when you heard about something momentous that has happened, such as the assassination of President John F. Kennedy or the September 11 attack on the twin towers in New York.

Irrespective of the neurological detail, however, the house with the flood works well as a simple model of memory and cognition, and for the purposes of this book, the negative thoughts refer to those that provide the themes for rumination. One way we could try to deal with these ruminative thoughts would be to block them out. In our house-of-the-mind analogy, this would be represented by keeping the door firmly shut where the flood is; we experience this as denial or avoidance.

Paradoxically, avoidance does work, but usually only as a short-term measure. In the long run, avoidance is a maladaptive way of responding because the pressure of suppressing emotions may simply overwhelm the effort to keep them at bay. In our house model, we could represent that as the flood breaking down the door and flooding the house of the mind. The trauma literature provides dramatic illustrations of the longer-term effects of avoidance, often in military contexts. After World War I, many returning veterans suffered from what was then called *shell shock*, a form of post-traumatic stress disorder (PTSD): the intrusion of ruminative memories of their experiences, which had been dealt with by denial, silence, and maintaining a "stiff upper lip." Some American veterans of the Vietnam War returned to civilian life seemingly unaffected until something happened to trigger a full-blown post-traumatic response, sometimes years later. What these case studies show is that out of sight is not out of mind. For victims of PTSD there has been no resolution of the emotional trauma.

This process of suppressing feelings is of course not only associated with trauma, as you'll surely have discovered yourself in ordinary working life when you've tried to push things aside. Unless the issues are resolved, they will eventually burst through the blockade, and when they provoke rumination, you end up overwhelmed and drowning in the flood of negative emotion. Avoidance is one of the key factors that make people less resilient, but it isn't something that everyone habitually engages in. A more common experience is that the negative emotion just bursts through, without any attempt to keep it out. Whether or not you've attempted to avoid the emotion, the outcome is the same: drowning in the flood of rumination.

These two options—avoidance and eventually being overwhelmed, or just being overwhelmed—seem to exhaust the possibilities, but there is a third one. First, though, we need to accept that it isn't possible to become mindless and emotionless: the flood will always be there. Resilience isn't the equivalent of finding the plug in the floor so the flood can drain away. But if the flood is always going to be there, how can we ever be free? In other words, with an ever-present flood, how can we avoid being overwhelmed when it bursts in?

There is a solution, but we need to add another dimension to our house of the mind by adding a loft or attic to it. We are just extending a metaphor, but once the loft has been added, the way to deal with the flood becomes clear. First, you open the door opposite the flood, and keep it open. Next, you open the door where the flood is, and you keep that open as well. Then you go upstairs into the loft, and the flood passes through below you. Being in the loft is what detachment means: being able to step back and see things for what they are without becoming involved in them. You're not denying the thoughts, but neither are you entertaining them with attention. Instead, you are taking attention from them and letting them go by coming back into the present. Negative thoughts are fed by attention, and when they're fed, they stay and grow. It's a bit like having unwelcome house guests—if you feed them, they stay; don't give them any food, and they'll soon leave!

You might be involved in the present in a project that starts to go wrong, but that's pressure, not stress. Your heart rate and blood pressure will go up, but that's entirely appropriate—you need the arousal to be awake enough to deal with the issue effectively. The question is whether you go on afterward ruminating about the what-ifs and if-onlys, which is the equivalent of thrashing around in the flood, not being able to see things for what they are.

Being able to keep everything in perspective and letting the negative thoughts go leads to freedom from the tyranny of rumination, but there is nonetheless a catch with our third diagram. When we ask what the catch might be, the answer usually involves wondering how to get up into the loft—are there stairs? To understand the model properly, it need not be taken too literally. The principle is this: you don't need any stairs; you stay permanently in the loft. Recall a recent bout of rumination, where the thoughts kept coming back into your mind, and each time they did, you elaborated on them and fed them with attention. After a week or so of having the thoughts return again and again, this time when it happens, you think, "Hang on, why am I bothering with that again?" What you've effectively said to yourself is, "This is an inconsequential thought that's just making me miserable." To be able to ask the question of yourself, you must have become detached and seen the thought for what it is: just a thought. Why would you ever want to lose that perspective? Using our model, one way of describing resilience is living permanently in the loft, from where things can be seen in their proper perspective.

The real catch with the house and the flood, though, is that the negative thoughts that you've let go have a habit of coming back around again! Isn't that your experience, that ruminating is a repetitious process? Round and round until it eventually recedes, but if you're a professional ruminator, it will take a long time, and when it does recede, it will quickly be replaced by the next worry. This is a habit, and like all habits, rumination is strengthened by doing it. When rumination does start, you can choose to avoid it, to feed it, or to wake up as soon as possible. When rumination starts, the thoughts suck your attention down into the nightmare of stress, and when they take hold, you create a virtual reality in your mind in which you are completely absorbed and back in the situation as if it were happening again. All nightmares are like this. Rumination is just another level of sleep, and like any nightmare, you can free yourself from it only by waking up.

Because of the strength of habit, we should expect the thoughts to return, so be prepared. The thoughts *will* come back. If you think this is an instant solution, you'll end up disappointed that it hasn't worked immediately and permanently. You might even start to think that letting go can't be done. The critical thing is how you respond when the negative thoughts do return. You have three choices: avoiding them, feeding them, or waking up. Once you do wake up, the opportunity is there to control attention and regain perspective by seeing them as just thoughts, which you can let go.

When negative thoughts return, there are three choices: avoiding them, feeding them, or waking up.

When people first start practicing, they often find they wake up only after rumination has returned and reestablished a firm grip.

Then they feel disappointed that it hasn't disappeared completely, but it doesn't actually matter if it does return. As we've said, this isn't the road to Damascus, and like everything that's worthwhile, it requires practice. With practice, the four steps eventually become second nature, and you'll hardly get caught by rumination at all.

Once you have woken up and taken control of attention, there is the opportunity to get things into perspective and to let go, but letting go doesn't mean doing nothing. What you let go of is not the task but the negative emotion that might accompany it. Most of what we do has an emotional component, so tasks come wrapped in emotion. This might be the passion and enthusiasm for doing them, which is useful, but it might equally be ruminative worry about not finishing in time or doing a poor job. Letting go of the negative emotion leaves a clear view of what needs to be done. Letting go isn't about putting your feet up. It's about doing the job without the contamination of negative emotion. This is why detachment is not just a form of avoidance. The thoughts do intrude into your mind, but instead of blocking them out or fixating on them, you're observing and acknowledging them as just thoughts, and you're letting go of them by not continuing to feed them with attention.

THE CONUNDRUM OF RUMINATION

If rumination is such a curse, why do people do it? You might say that it's just a habit, but why did the habit develop in the first place? We always ask training groups whether anyone in the audience has never ruminated, and no one raises his or her hand. Why do people engage in behavior that makes them so miserable and could be shortening their lives? When the question is posed, another response is to suggest that it is inevitable: "My father was a ruminator.

So was my mother, and so was my grandmother, so no wonder I do it as well." If this family history were a consequence of genetics, it would be inevitable, but while genetic predispositions probably play a role in most of our behavior, the genetic contribution to rumination is small. Otherwise, it would be impossible to change. The reason is more likely to be nurture, copied from the models that are presented to you.

A more common justification for rumination is thinking that you learn from it, but as we've pointed out, that comes from confusing rumination with reflection. A different way to understand what keeps the habit of ruminating in place is to consider who it is devoted to: who is the central character in all your rumination? The answer is "me," who is by turns all suffering or all conquering. When people feel stressed, it ends up feeling like "fortress me," with troops armed to the teeth and up on the battlements. Stress is an effortful, defensive process, but the paradox is that the fort can be demolished and the troops sent home—there's nothing to defend. "Me" is largely a figment of your imagination.

> *A common justification for rumination is thinking that you learn from it. You don't.*

An anecdote might help—not everyone will relate to it, but it's the principle that's important. Suppose you receive a bonus, and you decide to splurge on what you think is a really great outfit, but when you arrive at work the next day, the first colleague you meet takes one look and makes a derogatory remark about it. What happens to "me"? It slides into embarrassment, disappointment, and anger. Minutes later, a different colleague enthuses about how great you look and what good taste you have. "Me" swells with pride.

In other words, your emotions just go up and down depending on what people say. Here's the principle: for every 100 people you meet, more or less 25 will like you, more or less 25 won't, and more or less 50 will be in the middle, *but it doesn't matter.* These are just people's opinions. We spend a great deal of time engaged in what the sociologist Erving Goffman described as impression management, trying to get everybody to love "me," but it will never happen, and unless you want to spend your life at the mercy of opinion, it really doesn't matter.

This is not to say that you don't care about what anyone says. If your manager comments on a piece of work you did that wasn't up to standard but prefaces it with "You idiot!" this "me" character will most likely latch onto the preface, feel anger rising, ruminate, and even try to justify poor work. There's a useful lesson here: although expressing it in the way the manager did was completely inappropriate, and definitely not what you'd expect from a real leader, the work wasn't up to standard. By focusing on the real message and letting go of the emotional upset, there's an opportunity to learn and to change. You might need to take some action with regard to this manager, perhaps even changing jobs if the organization condones this kind of behavior, but all of your actions need to be done with detachment.

Once you take these negative opinions to heart and start to ruminate about the emotional upset, something has been completely hijacked: attention. When your subsequent actions are informed by anger and resentment, you've lost it, and actions informed by anger seldom have useful outcomes. Attention produces everything. Having a low opinion of yourself is all in the realm of "me," and it is a great mistake. The training program is essentially about *empowerment*, which is an overused term. What it really means is realizing that you have this amazing power of attention. Why allow it to be stolen away by pointless rumination?

THE FORCE IS WITH YOU

The way in which ruminative thoughts can compromise action is clearly illustrated in the science fiction film series Star Wars. Toward the end of *Episode IV: A New Hope* (first film in the series, released in 1977 as *Star Wars*), the Rebel Alliance is being threatened by the Death Star of the enemy Galactic Empire, commanded by Darth Vader. To survive, the Rebel Alliance has to bomb the Death Star, but the bomb has to be dropped down an awkward and narrow shaft. The Rebel Alliance has only three bombs. Luke Skywalker and two other attack craft, each carrying a bomb, head off on the mission. The two other pilots are shot down, and Skywalker is the Rebel Alliance's last hope. He slides into desperate rumination. All you can see is his face, but what he's thinking is obvious: "What if I miss? If only there were more bombs!"

Once you get into this state, you're bound to fail, but Skywalker is saved by the voice of his teacher Obi-Wan Kenobi. What Obi-Wan tells him is to wake up, control his attention, become detached, and let go. Of course, what he actually tells Luke Skywalker to do is to *use the Force*. The Force is attention. In fact, Obi-Wan explicitly tells him to use the Force by just letting go! Attention is available to you to focus where it's needed only when you let go of the contaminating ruminative thoughts. What you let go of isn't the task but the accompanying negative emotion. There's work to be done, but you can do something successfully only if attention is controlled, going into the past and the future intentionally to draw on experience and plan for outcomes, but with the present as the frame of reference.

What you let go of isn't the task but the accompanying negative emotion.

The Star Wars films are just sci-fi stories, but the Force is a perfect metaphor for attention: the power that gets everything done when you control and direct it rather than allowing it to be snatched away. The idea of the Force is also widely used in sports. You will often hear athletes talking about being "in the zone." You get into the zone by letting everything go and focusing on what is in front of you. The *zone* and the *present* are synonyms. To be an expert, you must have the skills that come from dedicated practice, but after that, successful performance in sports or anything else you engage in is all about mind—what athletes refer to as "the top two inches." To do anything successfully, having the right aptitude, skills, and passion are prerequisites, but these are of no value if waking sleep or rumination intervene and attention control is lost. Once the negative emotion that accompanies rumination enters, the consequence is stress. Freedom from stress follows from taking the four steps of waking up (and staying awake for as long as you can), controlling attention, becoming detached, and letting go.

Taking the four steps will liberate you personally from the tyranny of stress, but training participants often ask what they can do to help others who are stressed. First, you must be practicing the steps yourself. The most powerful way to teach is by example, and telling others not to be stressed won't work if you're a stress ball yourself. It is also important not to assume that people are stressed—it might just be your perception. More often than not, when people say how stressed they are, they're really just under a lot of pressure. So the next thing you can do is to use the language we're proposing in this book to distinguish between pressure and stress: are they ruminating? If they are, then they're stressed. More likely they're under a lot of pressure that they're misidentifying as stress. If you're someone who is able to keep things in perspective and doesn't go on worrying, it will be obvious to others, and these people might then approach you to find out how you do it. This is the ideal situation since they will have decided themselves to initiate change. Furthermore, because the program is so simple, it is relatively easy to explain. If you do get the opportunity to describe what it's about, it is equally important not to expect change, especially if you're a manager offering advice to a direct report. You know that habits can be difficult to shift, so you can't hold people to account for changing their behavior—you need to be as forgiving of them as you are of yourself.

What does it feel like to be resilient? Some people are resilient most of the time, but everyone has experienced it. Think back to the last time you went to work as usual and everything just seemed to flow: you did as much in one day as might otherwise take a week. You went to work the next day, and it felt like wading through molasses! Sometimes this is just tiredness, but if it isn't and if the amount of work at hand is the same as the previous day, you can be sure that your good day was marked by resilience. Rather than have that happen by chance, continued practice of the four steps can turn it into an intentional habit.

LIBERATED LEADERSHIP

A key challenge for high-performing leaders is how to strive for great results without getting overly attached to them. Become too attached to a fixed outcome and you'll be thrown by factors you can't control or disappointed by a result that works but doesn't meet your expectations. On the other hand, be too blasé about process and your team will lose direction and fail to deliver. The ability to maintain the balance is one that can take leaders years to learn, and many never do. One business owner we worked with gave this advice for how he was able to keep pushing for great results without getting stressed by it: "I discovered early in my career that if you don't learn to keep work in perspective and let things go, it will bury you."

Detachment is keeping things in perspective, and once you've done so, you can let go—not of the drive to succeed but of the attachment to the negative emotion that will turn that drive into stress. The good news is that both detachment and letting go are skills that can be learned, and as in previous leadership sections of our book we can contrast what skilled or unskilled leader behavior looks like:

Skilled in Resilience

- Put things in perspective by focusing on the values that matter most

- See the day-to-day pressures of work as non-life-threatening

- Handle other people's strong emotions without taking them on

- Differentiate between caring (useful) and worrying (useless)

- Use humor to break the tension in tough situations

- Know that change is continuous and shape it rather than resist it

- Help direct reports surface and let go of what is overwhelming them

- Let go of grudges and forgive quickly

- Are open-minded to new approaches and are not constrained by "how we did things in the past"

Unskilled in Resilience

- Catastrophize about how bad things will be if various events were to occur

- Blow situations out of proportion, making small events seem big

- Are often in emergency mode, as if everything is a crisis to manage

- Believe they will be unable to handle future events so ruminate to prepare for them

- Force their teams to overprepare for events that may or may not happen

- Take on other people's emotions and problems as their own

- Fuse their identity with their career, kids, finances

- Hold on to grudges and are slow to forgive and forget

- Relitigate past decisions even when there is no chance of overturning them

Here are six specific strategies for developing these skills.

1. Approach work with high intent, low attachment. All leaders need to work out for themselves and their teams how to set high standards without a fear of failure. Leaders who skillfully navigate this tension have what one of our colleagues calls an attitude of *high intent and low attachment.* Think of a surgeon whose *intent* is to have the best possible result for the patient, but he knows that he must stay *detached* and clearheaded throughout the operation. As a leader you can do this by asking, "What is my highest intent in this situation?" If the answer is to make a positive contribution in the meeting you're attending, then you do your best to have that impact without expecting or demanding that people react in exactly the way you want.

By focusing on your intent rather than a specific outcome, you acknowledge that there are many factors that impinge on your work that you can't control, which will enable you to pursue your intent without being held hostage by your attachment to the end result. What is the highest intent you have for your leadership?

2. Use humor to put work back in its place. Each day we're presented with people and events that, taken together, can convince us that our work is incredibly important. Occasionally we all need a reminder that puts it back in perspective. One manufacturing company we work with is full of driven individuals who are deeply committed to hitting their numbers, but when someone wakes up and realizes they're all starting to take it all too seriously, they'll say something like, "Guys, we make milk cartons!" There's a moment's hesitation before everyone laughs and goes back to their task, but awake and with a proper perspective.

A former faculty member at the Center for Creative Leadership (CCL) would remind staff who were losing control of attention and drifting into rumination that "there's no such thing as a leadership development *emergency!*" People just had to laugh as they tried to come up with scenarios that would constitute a leadership development emergency. A missing handout? Feedback delivered in the wrong order? The humor is not intended to make so light of the tasks that they're not done with care and attention, but there aren't many of us whose work is going to cure world hunger. Think about what you can say to yourself and what you can say to your team when people start losing perspective about work.

3. Compare the current situation to your life experiences. Sometimes we end up ruminating because we forget how small the current issue is in the scope of our whole life. One of the fastest ways we see leaders get out of rumination is by contrasting a current event (an unhappy colleague) with bigger, tougher, more consequential events they have gone through in their lives.

One of our engineering clients hires a lot of military veterans, and in workshops they tell us that when they are having a tough day, they remind themselves that this doesn't compare to a tough day in combat. Other people tell us that that they remind themselves of major illnesses they have gone through, or other tough periods in their lives. The *contrast* has the effect of immediately shrinking events back to their appropriate size. What are the events that have happened in your life that you can use to keep the daily stuff in proper perspective?

4. Ask yourself three questions when you are in a crisis. People who struggle to detach often ask themselves very unhelpful questions: "Why did this happen to me?" "Why can't I be more successful?" To break that habit, ask yourself these questions instead:

> *Question 1.* "What's **funny** about this?" When I (Nick) became ill with cancer in my twenties, I found myself asking, "Why me?" and there seemed to be nothing funny about it. I then remembered what happened when my brother visited me in the hospital, made some smart, sarcastic comment, and promptly fainted! Despite the circumstances, that was funny!

> *Question 2.* "What's **great** about this?" Again, I could see nothing great about having cancer, but then it became clear to me: "This is the toughest challenge I will ever face. If I

can get through this, I'll be strong enough to get through anything else life brings."

Question 3. "What's the **opportunity** here?" This one was easier: "Stop wasting my life, find a career that allows me to make a significant positive contribution to others, and since I don't know how long I've got, get as good at it as quickly as possible." Not knowing how long you've got is true for everyone, so don't waste it ruminating! However long you have, the only time you can act is now, which is why Challenge of Change Resilience Training emphasizes acting in the present. The quality of your life and leadership is a lot about the quality of the questions you ask yourself right now: there is always something about every situation that is funny, great, and opportune. The challenge is whether or not you ask the right questions to uncover them.

5. Clarify who actually owns the problem. One behavior that is guaranteed to start you ruminating is failing to differentiate between other people's problems and your own. Imagine a direct report comes into your office complaining about the unjustness of an upcoming organizational change. An ineffective leader will often fall into one or the other extreme: dismiss the issue to avoid getting involved in the person's emotions, or he will sympathize completely and in the process end up taking on the anger as well. The most effective leaders begin by seeing that the other person owns the problem, not them. They listen with full attention, enabling the person to express fully how upset he or she feels. Then they ask smart questions to help guide the best actions to follow, but when the person leaves the room, any emotions they are still holding leave as well.

Many leaders we know have worked out how to do this in the office, but they go home to their families and do exactly the opposite. They take ownership of their teenager's grades and of their partner's rumination. At home, it's personal. We get it, and that is exactly why you need to be extra vigilant at home about detaching from that which is not yours. When dealing with a partner, ask yourself, "Did my partner actually ask me to solve this problem for her?" If the answer is no, then stop "helping" so much. If the answer is no but you still feel compelled to get involved, then she doesn't have a problem. You do. And kids are smart: as long as you're taking responsibility for their problems, they don't need to!

6. Teach your teams how to use SBI Feedback. One reason many people find it hard to let go is because they feel an emotion, but they don't know how to express it appropriately. To help leaders resolve this problem, the Center for Creative Leadership teaches a method called Situation, Behavior, and Impact (SBI) Feedback, which is delivered in three simple steps:

> *Situation.* Describe the precise time and place where the behavior occurred (for example, "in our client meeting this morning").

> *Behavior.* Say what the person did or said (for example, "You told the clients that I would fly back to meet them anytime they wanted").

> *Impact.* Say how you felt as a result (for example, "I was surprised and felt concerned").

This method works well because it avoids trying to second-guess what the other person's intentions were and coming to conclusions that may be informed more by emotional attachment than rational problem solving (such as thinking it was an attempt to undermine you). Instead, the strategy aims at objectivity: "Here are your behaviors, and this is how I felt as a result." This provides a bridge to a conversation in which the two parties can learn whether the impact they *intended* to have matches the impact they *actually* had. SBI enables emotional expression in the context of a detached perspective, and it facilitates letting go of the emotions and moving forward, often with a stronger relationship as a result (for more see www.youtube.com/watch?v=Sk79WxURKtU).

CASES IN POINT

Cricketers

Keith Miller was a famous Australian cricketer who had his career interrupted by World War II. He joined the Royal Air Force (RAF) as a fighter pilot and battled the German Luftwaffe. Miller survived many dangerous missions, and when the war ended, he returned to Australia and began playing cricket for his country again.

During a press conference, a reporter asked him how he coped with the intensity and pressure of playing international sports. Miller looked at the reporter and then burst out laughing. "What pressure? Pressure is flying over Germany at 10,000 feet with a German Messerschmitt up your ass. This is a game, mate!"

Statesmen

In 1962 a 27-year-old man was arrested. His cause was just, but he was sent to jail for life, leaving behind a wife and young family. Twenty-seven years later, he was released. Given the circumstances and all he had lost, how hard would it be to forgive and let go?

When Nelson Mandela was released from prison, many expected him to exact retribution against the white ruling class, and people were braced for a bloody civil war. But he decided to take another path. In an epic quote he said, "As I walked out the door toward the gate that would lead to my freedom, I knew if I didn't leave my bitterness and hatred behind, I would remain in prison." Mandela decided to set an example for all South Africans. "If I can do it, so can you."

HOW TO CASCADE RESILIENCE THROUGHOUT THE ORGANIZATION

One question organizational leaders often ask is how they can cascade these resilience-building tools efficiently to their teams on the front lines. For example, one company we worked with was going through difficult times because of historically low commodity prices in its industry. The company wanted the most senior leaders not only to develop their own resilience but also that of the people they led. Because of the tough economic situation, the CEO's leadership team didn't have the resources to train everyone in the company, but they knew their people needed help.

To help them achieve this goal, we began with resilience workshops for the top 120 leaders so that all senior executives would be equipped with the tools. We held three workshops over three days, which meant that leaders had a choice of when to attend and the organization could continue to run smoothly. Each session was introduced by a member of the CEO's leadership team to emphasize the importance of the training.

To cascade the ideas from the training out to even more people, the organization and the Center for Creative Leadership implemented an approach called Each One Teach One. This meant that each leader who attended the session would teach the new tools to one group of people—in this case, his team. A series of short videos explained the concepts and tools. The leader and his team watched these videos as a group and then went through a guided discussion about how they could apply the new concepts as a group.

Within two months, nearly a thousand employees were exposed to the new Challenge of Change Resilience Training concepts. Words such as *rumination* and *wake up* became catalysts for discussion and change; *resilience* became not just a training module but a central part of the company vernacular. Ongoing check-in sessions that leaders created for their teams offered a safe context in which people could voice their views and concerns, and feedback from these sessions was incorporated into company well-being strategies. The pressure from the economic uncertainty continued, but the resilience tools helped employees cope much more effectively and keep performing despite a tough period for the company.

SUMMARY

- Having woken up and regained control of attention, the next step is to become detached.

- In this book, the word *detached* is used to describe the ability to keep issues in perspective, rather than the more conventional idea of being disengaged or not caring.

- You can only reflect once you've become detached, so to really care requires detachment.

- In our house metaphor for the mind, the doors to the house need to be left open so it can all flow through, observed by you from the detached position of the loft of the house.

- Letting it flow through and not attaching to any of it is the last step of letting go.

- Tasks come wrapped in emotion, and what you let go of is the wrapping—the negative emotion. That leaves the task, which you can then attend to without your judgment being clouded by waking sleep or rumination.

- As a resilient leader, you can help your teams do the following:

- Approach work with high intent and low attachment.

- Use humor to put things in perspective.

- Compare the current situation to life experiences to gain perspective.

  - Ask three questions about the situation: "What is funny about this?" "What is great about this?" "What is the opportunity here?"

- Clarify who actually owns the problem.

- Teach teams how to use Situation, Behavior, and Impact (SBI) Feedback.

5

DEVELOPING
A RESILIENT
PERSONALITY

Changing ruminative behavior is achieved by practicing the four steps outlined in the previous chapters, though a further refinement was added by including differences in whether people expressed or inhibited their emotions. Rumination and emotional inhibition were the first two psychometric measures to emerge from the research, but subsequent work uncovered a total of eight different habitual behaviors that all contribute in some degree to making people more or less resilient. Of the eight measures, rumination is the most important. The second most important is detached coping, which forms the foundation for the third step in the program described in Chapter 4. We've also referred briefly to two other measures, emotional inhibition (Chapter 3) and avoidance coping (Chapter 4).

Specially designed versions of all eight scales are grouped into the psychometric Challenge of Change Resilience Profile that training participants complete as part of the program, and a substantial amount of time in the session is spent debriefing the profile, describing each of the measures and showing how they can be changed. The profile items and scores are not available outside of scheduled sessions. This is partly to ensure the protection of the intellectual property of the work, but it is done also because it would be unethical to provide a profile of scores that may have significant implications for an individual's well-being, with no opportunity for discussion about them. The behaviors that characterize the scales are described in detail in this chapter, and if you recognize features of them in yourself that you feel you need to change, each description is followed by pointers on what you can do about it.

DEFINING PERSONALITY

The way people behave is often referred to as "their personality" with the implicit assumption that it can't be changed. Personality is often thought of as hardwired, but there is no reason to make that assumption. The extent to which behavior can be changed is a function of whether it is either learned or determined biogenetically. *Personality* is a generic term used to indicate individual differences, without the additional qualification of how it is determined. Given the evidence we have for change in the measures we'll be describing, we regard these as measures of personality that are determined primarily by conditioning or learning, which is a key assumption: there would be no point in offering training to develop resilience if it were hardwired rather than a skill that can be acquired. In our view, personality can definitely change.

The different measures of resilience are grounded in psychometric scales, and when they're used in the training, they're prefaced by two important points. The first is a general caution about overinterpreting psychometric scales. As we've said, they are subject to bias, and even with the extent of the validation invested in the profile scales, they are not some kind of crystal ball. The second point is that they are determined primarily by nurture rather than nature: they represent habitual behavior, and habits can be changed. We've already acknowledged that there's probably DNA lurking in nearly all behavior, but from the evidence, there seem to be only two aspects of personality that are to a fairly large extent genetically determined: extraversion and emotionality. The strongest biogenetic evidence is for extraversion, but we know that extraversion is not implicated in resilience so it will not be described here. We did find that one specific dimension of emotionality—emotional sensitivity—was implicated. It forms one of the dimensions of the profile and is included in this chapter, though our research has again shown that this dimension of emotionality can be changed with practice.

EIGHT KEY PSYCHOMETRIC MEASURES OF RESILIENCE

The behaviors that characterize the profile scales are described in detail in this part of this chapter, and they are organized within the following eight categories:

1. Rumination

2. Emotional inhibition

3. Toxic achieving

4. Avoidance coping

5. Perfect control

6. Detached coping

7. Sensitivity

8. Flexibility

Rumination

What it looks like. Rumination was described in detail in Chapter 3. To summarize, in our continuum of sleep, rumination occurs when negative emotion is added to what we call *waking sleep*. It involves continuing to churn over emotional upsets, which prolongs the emotional misery as well as sustaining a perfectly natural physiological response to the point at which it may incur real damage. Rumination isn't a by-product of stress. It is stress. If there's no rumination, there's no stress.

How to change. You discover that you've been absent in a ruminative nightmare only when you wake up—the realization is always retrospective. This might seem paradoxical, but remember that waking sleep and rumination are simply extensions of what we ordinarily call *sleep*, and setting aside the lucid dreaming that some people experience, you know you've been dreaming only when you wake up. Because rumination is habitual, we find ourselves lapsing back into it, but now that you've been made aware of these lapses of attention and what they involve, waking up *will* happen. The key is to avail yourself of the opportunity to stay awake for as long as you can every time you do wake up: keep control of attention by connecting with your senses and focusing on what's in front of you. Staying awake reinforces the habit of waking up rather than just going back to sleep, and with practice, you'll wake up more frequently and be able to stay awake for longer periods of time. There is no magic bullet. There never is: change happens by first gaining understanding and then steadfastly putting change into practice.

Emotional Inhibition

What it looks like. Emotional inhibition measures the extent to which you bottle up or inhibit emotion. It isn't a measure of how much emotion you experience; everyone experiences emotion. It is whether or not you express it. The context in which you have the opportunity to express emotion is your social support network, which at one time was assessed very simply by the number of people available to you. People who habitually inhibit their feelings are unlikely to avail themselves of the opportunity. What is more important is your *willingness* to disclose, and this is an important component of our scale.

There are circumstances in which it isn't appropriate to say how you feel. For example, people working in the emergency services have to deal with extremely traumatic situations, but they are required to treat whatever they encounter as being part of the job and just get on with it. One of the consequences is that not expressing how they feel can become an occupational hazard, as we saw earlier with war veterans who suffered from undiagnosed post-traumatic stress. Emergency services staff use strategies such as black humor to deflect the impact of trauma, which can be shocking to bystanders, but they are also routinely given the opportunity for debriefing sessions after major events. These are a formalized version of social support, and they have become part of the standard approach to helping anyone exposed to trauma, but it remains the case that you have to be willing to say how you feel for it to be effective.

A simple way of illustrating the benefit of emotional expression is to remember an occasion when you had an emotional issue and the opportunity arose to tell someone about it. This person might be a friend or a professional counselor, but if you did take the opportunity, you'll know that it provided an unburdening effect. One way it might help is as a way of getting specific practical advice, but mainly what it does is help you gain perspective: the act of speaking about something has the effect of making it separate from you, rather than just being in your mind. The story you tell isn't all that important. It's the extent to which you express how you feel that has the effect: in post-trauma counseling sessions, people are encouraged to preface what they say with "I feel" rather than "I think."

Expressing emotion is not an end in itself. The purpose is to help you reach a resolution to what's bothering you. This doesn't necessarily mean that you will reach a definite solution—if someone has died, no amount of grieving will bring him or her back—but we're able to begin to acknowledge that everyone dies. Bereavement counseling is not about gaining resolution as rapidly as possible, and for some, the process may take years to work through. However, for the kinds of everyday issues that we're addressing in this book, resolution can be achieved much more quickly than if feelings are bottled up. In other words, you're much more quickly able to let go.

Expressing emotion is not an end in itself. The purpose is to help you reach a resolution to what's bothering you.

There is an important caveat to expressing emotion, which is that you need to make sure the time and place are appropriate—it isn't an invitation to blurt it all out wherever you are! We all know people who endlessly whine about their problems, and because it's usually the same old things they're complaining about, they're clearly not getting to any resolution. They've become verbal ruminators. The purpose of expressing emotion is to help you move on, which they're not doing.

Another caveat is that among the scales we've developed, emotional inhibition is the one where there is a significant bias: on average, using large random samples, men are significantly more likely than women to inhibit emotion. The findings fit with the broad stereotype of women as being more willing to say how they feel, and it turns out to be very protective: women tend to live on average up to five years longer than men do. There are many factors that contribute to the effect, but research suggests that the tendency to express rather than inhibit emotion also plays a role. The reason for the gender difference has provoked endless speculation about nature versus nurture. There are probably genetic factors at play—there almost always are!—but it is equally true that from a young age, boys have traditionally been taught that saying how they feel is a weakness.

Taking rumination and inhibition together, the preferred pattern of scores on the psychometric profile is to have low scores on both—in other words, to express emotion appropriately and not to ruminate. If people do ruminate but also tend to express how they feel, that can be helpful to the extent that although they ruminate more than most, the effect is mitigated by the perspective that is gained whenever they do unburden. There are those who score relatively low on rumination but never say how they feel, which is, not surprisingly, found more often among men than women. While they don't incur the emotional and physiological costs of habitual rumination, it can be hard work for others trying to figure out how they feel. The most problematic pattern, though, is being a ruminator who bottles up emotion. In our lab experiments we were able to isolate the effects for each of the measures separately and together, and using measures like how long it took people's heart rate and blood pressure to recover after being exposed to stress, we found that nonexpressive ruminators took the longest to recover of any of the groups.

How to change. If you recognize that you do tend to inhibit emotion, are you doing so because of a *fear of disclosure*, the feeling that opening up will leave you vulnerable and exposed, or experiencing embarrassment when someone else does it? This comes from a mistaken all-or-none idea, that if you don't keep your emotions to yourself, then every conversation is going to turn into a full-blown counseling session. Well, feel the fear and act against it. At the next team meeting when you feel upset about something, say so, but say it from a detached perspective.

Starting to change emotional inhibition can be easier by involving someone whom you can trust sufficiently to acknowledge that you'd like to change, and then trying it out in the safety of that relationship. For example, in one of our training sessions, it emerged that one man had the maximum score on this scale. This was a team session in which scores were being shared, and he realized how much of an effect it had on other members of his team. Having acknowledged the problem, and wanting to change, he was given a task to help with this. He was married, so the task was to find an opportunity when he got home to have a conversation with his wife, starting with him saying that he didn't express emotion enough. When he did this, she replied, "Tell me about it!" He went on to talk about how he *felt* about what he had done that day—not just what he had done, which he could easily talk about, but how he felt about it.

Because he was working against habit, he didn't find this easy—like most habits, it's the thought of doing something different that deters us from trying—but he persisted, and over time the effect was significant. He didn't become a heart-on-the-sleeve discloser, but being so much more comfortable talking about how he felt made his relationships at work and at home much easier.

Toxic Achieving

What it looks like. Have you ever had a manager who placed you under constant time pressure to get things done, didn't really care how you got a result as long you got one, and responded to any failure to deliver with impatience and anger? These managers are probably not all that common, but working for them is such a negative experience they're difficult to forget. One of our measures taps into these characteristics, which we call *toxic achieving*.

Instructions from these toxic achievers are always couched as, "I needed it yesterday." They think the end justifies the means, and their tendency to anger makes everyone afraid of them. They also tend to be clever manipulators, and they will often cultivate favorites in the team: divide and rule. If all of this behavior sounds psychopathic, to some extent it is.

A helpful way of thinking about behavior, normal or abnormal, is that it tends toward a bell-shaped curve. This is the basis for the idea of a spectrum, where someone might have a tendency toward some of the symptoms that characterize a condition like Asperger's syndrome, but not all of them, so that person's condition would lie toward the middle of the spectrum. The same idea is applied to other illnesses as well: people with some of the symptoms of schizophrenia might be considered schizotypic.

It would be wrong to suggest, as some have, that toxic achieving managers are psychopaths—psychopathy is a much more complex issue than being an unpleasant boss. However, they certainly share some of the characteristics of psychopathy, including being extremely self-serving—these are managers who will take credit when things go well but will be quick to attribute blame when they don't. What motivates toxic achieving behavior is the mistaken belief that threats and blame will get work done, and the most difficult aspect of toxic achievers is the second word in the phrase: they *do* deliver, which is why they're often successful. They're also consummate self-promoters, so they make their successes known to everyone in the organization.

The catch is that they deliver at significant cost not only to themselves but to their teams. Their people do a good job because they're told to, not because they respect their manager. Dissatisfaction and turnover tend to be high on these teams. The paradox is that you can actually deliver better if your drive to achieve is *not* expressed in a toxic manner. The cost to toxic achievers themselves is the cardiovascular strain that the impatience and anger bring in their train. Our interest in toxic achievers came originally from our study of a well-known concept, the *type A behavior pattern* (TABP). Compared to type Bs, type As were considered to be coronary-prone, though confusingly, they appeared not to be in controlled trials. The problem turned out to be with the measurement of TABP, which was psychometrically flawed. This led us to develop a measure that distinguished accurately between those who showed the behavior pattern and those who did not. On our measure, high scorers on toxic achieving correspond in some respects to type As, and low scorers to type Bs, but the TABP scales provided a flawed index of coronary-proneness. Although being a toxic achiever incurs significant health risks, toxic achieving has a wider focus that includes attitudes and behavior.

We've been using toxic achieving exclusively in the context of a management style, but it doesn't just characterize differences between managers. It can just as easily be the way team members behave, putting unnecessary pressure on themselves to get things done, cutting corners to get those results, and getting angry with themselves or their colleagues when things don't work out. Although the impact on the team might not be as marked as it is when managers behave in this way, the climate of the team is bound to be affected. The personal costs in terms of sustained physiological demand apply irrespective of the individual's position on the team, and resilience is significantly compromised by toxic achieving behavior.

How to change. Changing toxic achieving behavior is made more difficult by its success in getting tasks done, which makes it much easier to justify. If you're always responding to frustration with anger, notice how you'll tend to justify that anger to yourself and to others. Here are good questions to ask yourself: "Why am I always angry? And why do I think everyone, including me, should be delivering everything yesterday, at whatever cost to anyone else who might be involved? Why am I so identified with being tough?"

Toxic achievers make the same mistake as people afraid of disclosure, casting everyone into two extreme positions: you're either tough, or you're a weak softie. There's a simple exercise to show yourself what the costs are: portable battery-powered blood-pressure monitors are easily obtained and operated, so get one and take your own blood pressure when you're relaxed and contented (rare moments for toxic achievers), and then think about the last time you were in one of your habitual angry, blaming modes. Take it again as soon as possible after one of these little nuclear explosions of yours. Shocked? Hopefully. Change sometimes needs a jolt to get it going. And how often are you like this? You're bound to have colleagues you think of as being soft. Do they deliver less than you? And is their team happier than yours? The answers are no and yes. Constantly putting people under hostile pressure doesn't get them to work any more efficiently, and anger leads to a fearful, blaming culture.

> *Toxic achievers make the mistake of casting*
> *everyone into two extremes:*
> *you're either tough or you're a weak softie.*

One of the problems with justifying our behavior is that it ensures it will continue. The obstacle is in starting to make the change. One way you can help yourself is to make it public. Having decided you need and want to change, put it on the agenda for the next team meeting. Toxic achieving is a habit to which you've become addicted, so take a leaf from Alcoholics Anonymous: "Hi, I'm John, and I'm a toxic achiever." You'll certainly have everyone's attention! It takes courage to do this, so remind your colleagues and reports that they shouldn't expect an instantaneous transformation. Changing habits takes time, but ask them to let you know next time they see the red mist. Does your courage match your anger?

Avoidance Coping

What it looks like. In Chapter 4 we described the strategy that some use when faced with a problem: avoidance coping. Depending on how you define *coping*, avoidance isn't really coping at all since it involves burying your head in the sand and hoping the issue will just go away. The problem with this strategy is that nothing is resolved. In the trauma literature there are innumerable examples of the consequences of avoidance: people apparently managing fine, when in fact all they're doing is suppressing their responses. As we've said, this might work in the short term, but it takes only a trigger of some sort, often not even related to the original event, for all of the avoided emotion to rush back into the mind. When it does return, there's been no resolution, and these people can end up suffering from a full-blown post-traumatic response that was delayed for years.

This example of the dangers of avoidance comes from the traumatic end of the distribution. The focus of this book is on our day-to-day experiences, so a useful starting point is to ask why we might avoid dealing with things. There are many clichés to describe the "what" of it, such as certain items being in the too-hard basket, but why are they there? Viewed from the opposite perspective, why are some things never there? Suppose you have kids at school, and today's your turn to collect them. You might not want to interrupt what you're doing, but you nonetheless make sure you are there when school finishes because if you aren't, there could be significant personal consequences. Or perhaps you're studying a report you've been asked to review. You're finding it hard going, and since this isn't your department, you might feel that it doesn't really involve you anyway. Completing the review would be much easier to avoid than collecting your kids. If you don't turn up in time to collect the kids, they'll be upset and so will the school and probably your partner. If you don't complete the review, your colleagues will be upset and probably angry that you don't seem to care, but that's the point—you don't care enough about the emotional consequences to feel motivated to do it. The outcome is likely to be the same as the one we described in the previous section: you create the opportunity for another team to see you (and probably by default, your team) as the enemy. We all have to do things we'd prefer not to, and the consequence is that we use the wrong metric to evaluate and prioritize: an emotional index instead of a pragmatic, rational one.

As with almost everything we do, it is the intensity of the emotion that makes the difference, though the things we're most likely to avoid are at the ends of the intensity distribution. We can easily avoid what we don't really care about, but the too-hard basket might be just that. Think how difficult it is to deal with firing a direct report you know and like. It's no wonder people are sometimes fired by e-mail, or they find out about the likely effects of a drastic restructuring only from the rumor mill. The message for managers is to take the four steps in the training program, especially the last two: if something has to be done, keep it in perspective, and let go of the negative emotion that leads you to avoid the issue. Remember that detachment doesn't mean not caring. It needs to be linked directly to our measure of sensitivity: difficult issues need detached compassion.

How to change. When people engage in avoidance coping, they will also often justify and rationalize what they're doing: "I'll just put this aside for now, but I will come back to it," "This stuff isn't really all that important. I'll put it aside for the meantime." We may not actually think in these specific terms, but what we are doing is making it look like a rational response when it isn't. The key to dealing with avoidance is to recognize that it's an *emotional* response to things you'd prefer not to deal with. The paradox with avoidance is that for many of the things you put off until you eventually have to do them, you often find it is so straightforward and simple that you wonder what the fuss was all about. The issues don't change and become simpler because you avoided them for so long. Why go through all that, alienating people in the process, when you could just have done it when it first arrived?

We usually justify our avoiding behavior, to ourselves and everyone else, as the result of our being too busy. What we're really saying is that we're far too important to be bothering with this trivial stuff. Of course, you may well be too busy and genuinely not have the time to attend, but make the decision a rational one rather than an egocentric and emotional one. It isn't unusual to have several simultaneous demands on our time, but you can't give your attention to more than one novel task at a time. People described as multitaskers are very skilled at shifting their attention very rapidly between tasks, so it appears that they're doing more than one thing at a time. However, sometimes you need to prioritize and decide which task you're going to focus on. The others are parked in the meantime. The question you need to ask yourself is whether you think they're somehow going to disappear if you don't attend to them. That's avoidance. If you've put them aside and know you're going to return to them when you've completed the task at hand, that's strategic, and it is what we've called *reflection*.

*We usually justify our avoiding behavior
as the result of our being too busy.*

Avoidance fueled by emotion clouds our judgment, and we lose control of our attention. Procrastination is more the thief of attention than the thief of time. Whatever task you have to deal with, the principle is to do it or throw it away. This requires a wakeful reflective decision. You may not feel confident about deciding to trash something, but if you're unsure, the simplest solution is to check with your manager or team leader as to whether or not it really is important. The crucial step, though, is to see clearly for yourself the way that emotion creeps in to make your decisions seem reasonable.

Perfect Control

What it looks like. The idea of perfect control might sound very attractive, but it is in fact a major contributor to people being unhappy at work! We were led to it in our research by exploring the role of perfectionism. The problem for perfectionists is that they just can't see the *threshold of added value*, the point in the task beyond which you're adding nothing, no matter how much more detail you attend to. Perfectionism is based on the mistaken idea that there is a perfect outcome for the job. Everything can be improved upon; that's how we progress. More important, perfectionists never actually achieve this illusory perfection: no matter how much they do, they always feel they haven't done enough. Perfectionists consistently set the bar unrealistically high. Since there is very rarely a perfect outcome, perfectionism provides constant opportunities for them to beat themselves up for having "failed."

Like avoidance coping, perfect control is driven by emotion—in this case, anxiety. Perfect controllers are anxious about not delivering the perfect outcome, but they're struggling to achieve an ideal. There isn't a perfect result: everything can be improved upon. The consequence of perfectionism is that you'll always feel that you've failed, and the problem is that this attitude generalizes to our expectations of others as well. As with changing any of our behavior, we first have to recognize that we do it, and that can be difficult because of the way we rationalize what we do. Try telling perfectionists that what they've done so far on a project is good enough; they'll think you're settling.

This is not an argument for cutting corners or accepting substandard work, but rather, it is an approach to tasks that acknowledges the constraints of what can be achieved. In high-pressure environments we're seldom able to spend as long as we would like on any given piece of work, and we're not usually able to just throw more and more money into it. In fact, we don't even need to, since 80 percent of task outcomes are derived from 20 percent of the effort devoted to them. This is the well-known 80/20 rule, originally noted by the economist Vilfredo Pareto and applied specifically to work situations by Joseph Duran. Like all applied principles, it needs to be interpreted with caution, but it can best be visualized by a graph that plots effort against achievement. This will be a curve, with a steep gain in achievements initially, but the curve levels off to the point where more and more effort no longer yields significant gains.

How to change. From a practical perspective, the principle is to do the best you're able to under the circumstances, which is what most people do. The anxiety that drives perfectionism inevitably brings with it is a desire to control everything. So many people say that what stresses them out is not being in control. Well, there are things you can control or influence, but the world is an uncertain place, and there's a limit to how much control you have over it. Just consider for a moment how many of the projects you've been involved in have proceeded absolutely smoothly, without any hitches, exactly as you had planned them! We're talking about whether you can deliver a project by a deadline, when there are aspects you can control but others you probably can't, such as your needing to wait for another team to complete their part of the process before you can continue. This is why the final step in the training program, letting go, is particularly relevant for perfect controllers—being able to let go of the need to control what they can't control.

Having to delay a project is of course frustrating, but when that frustration turns to anger and labeling the other team as a bunch of slackers, the cooperative unity that is the hallmark of successful organizations is lost. There are things in the world you can control and things you can't, and you need to let go of the anger and blaming that feeds toxic achieving and rumination. More important, you need to remember that there is one thing that in principle you have control over at all times, and that's your attention. When we say that people have "lost it," what they've lost is control of their attention. Realizing you have control over attention means that you can give it selectively. You have a choice. You can indulge your frustration and allow it to turn to anger, at which point the other team that you're supposed to be working with will have become the enemy. Good organizations thrive on a sense of everyone's working with a common purpose; teamwork isn't just within teams but also among teams. The rational alternative choice is to recognize that all teams, including yours, encounter problems they have to solve. Frustration, inevitably yes; anger and blame, only if you mistakenly choose them and feed them with attention.

Team leaders have a significant role to play, though it does of course require that they not be perfectionists! Set a clear example for the *threshold of added value* for your reports, and make it clear that when people go beyond it, they're not only not adding any further value. Rather, they're compromising the delivery of the project. There is a balance to be struck because you want to ensure that the work does reach the threshold, and it will vary from one situation to another. It might also require drastic action. One of the managers we worked with had several perfect-control people on her team, which had the effect of making the others feel that they too had to act that way. Eventually, she introduced a rule: unless it was absolutely imperative, 5:30 p.m. was the time to go home. Then she would go around actually turning off the lights until they got the message!

Detached Coping

What it looks like. Developing a detached way of responding to the world is the third of the four steps in Challenge of Change Resilience Training, and the detached coping measure was referred to in Chapter 4. We now need to flesh out that description. As we've said, people will often interpret *detachment* as distancing oneself or not caring, but that's not what we mean. To be able to deal with anything, whether it is an abstract problem or someone's needing your help, you can't respond by distancing yourself. Detachment is the opposite: you can deal effectively with issues only by being detached and at the same time engaged, though to fully understand what that means, we will add a further dimension to it—*detached compassion*—when we get to the sensitivity index later in this chapter.

Detached coping is being able to keep perspective. Detached people don't turn molehills into mountains: they don't catastrophize, even when the issues are large and pressing. People often think they're solving problems by ruminating about them, but rumination is a repetitious cycle that solves nothing. In one sense, rumination is a very laudable green behavior, endlessly recycling garbage. To be free to act appropriately, we need to let go of the negative emotion we've unnecessarily added. This doesn't mean being unemotional, which is, in any case, impossible. Working under pressure is emotional, as we all know from the experience of collapsing in a heap when we get to the end of the project, but the emotion is positive and constructive instead of destructive. This is why to be able to reflect, we have to be detached. Genuine problem solving is reflection, drawing on past experience to generate solutions and waiting to see how well they actually work in the future.

How to change. Let's use a simple example to illustrate the practice of detachment. Your team is working happily on a complex but solvable issue for a client. The team leader is at an executive meeting and sends a text to say that everything's changed—the client wants to bolt a whole new component onto the project, and to complicate the issue, it has to be completed at the end of this week rather than the original time frame of next week. A final note in the text reminds the team that this is one of the company's most important clients, so to make sure that everything gets done well and on time. Detachment is a learned habit that will be distributed randomly across team members. At one extreme, at least some will be thrown into a panic, saying it can't be done and starting to ruminate about the dire consequences for the team. Panic is contagious, so others who might ordinarily be able to keep some perspective may get drawn into it.

The more panic and rumination, the less likely you are to meet the deadline, but if the team is fortunate enough to have even one member who can maintain detachment, this person's response will be along the lines of, "Hold on. Let's just think this through. If we can focus on the core issue, the overall solution should follow, so let's start with that. We should be able to deliver by Friday." This is not the same as brushing it off and thinking that the team managed it last time so it will be fine, and whatever happens was meant to be. Fatalism is as fatal as panic. Like panic, though, detachment is contagious, and it can have as much influence on the team as catastrophizing.

Fatalism is as fatal as panic.

All it needs is one person to be awake, someone who is keeping control of his or her attention and offering a clear way forward. Having the knowledge of the four steps in the program, you can be that person. One of the greatest advantages of being awake is being able to see things clearly, including the workings of your own mind, and being awake and detached allows you to evaluate the range of responses you could make and to choose the route you take. If this sounds too deliberate and calculating, the opposite is being an automaton, blindly acting on habit. One reason why people are reluctant to practice detachment is a concern that they'll be seen by others as unfeeling. The thing is that people are making judgments about us all the time—good, bad, and indifferent. They're all just opinions, and while they shouldn't be ignored, consider the costs of emotional catastrophizing: catastrophic responses, catastrophic decisions.

Sensitivity

What it looks like. One potential disadvantage of being detached is not that you don't care but that you might become so focused on dealing with a particular problem that you fail to adequately take other people's feelings about issues into account. Picking up quickly and accurately on how others feel forms another of the measures that comprise resilience. We call this *sensitivity*. We sometimes describe it as being able to know what was being talked about before you entered the room—that's an exaggeration, but it does give you a sense of what's involved.

Detachment and sensitivity are linked: if you are able to remain detached, it is equally important that you have sufficient sensitivity to be able to read the emotional tone of those you're working with. We describe this pattern as *detached compassion*. This might sound contradictory, but it is perfectly possible to be both at once. For example, suppose you're a professional counselor, and a client tells you about a catalog of distressing events that has happened to her. If you are low on detachment but high on sensitivity, you will probably identify with everything that's being described. Now there are two people with the problem instead of just the client, and nobody is helped by that. On the other hand, if you are very detached but lack sensitivity, you're not likely to relate to your client's suffering, and she isn't going to be helped at all.

* *

Detached compassion is empathy.

* *

Compassion means understanding the client's suffering. When that's coupled with detachment, it means knowing that it isn't you who is suffering. Identifying with other people's problems is called *sympathy*, and sympathy isn't helpful. A synonym for *detached compassion* is *empathy*. It is only from this perspective that you can help anyone at all. We've used counseling to illustrate the process, but this isn't just about counseling. Detached compassion is the way to live your life, at home as well as at work.

Sensitivity to others' emotions might be clouded by a combination of not being aware of them or by being completely preoccupied with your own feelings. Once you've woken up, controlled your attention, and become detached, you have the opportunity to see that life isn't a play written with you always at center stage. The program emphasizes the importance of both detached coping and sensitivity, and it doesn't take much reflection to appreciate the difference between being with people who have detached compassion and those who don't! Sensitivity is not hardwired, and it can be acquired by the practice of letting go of the preoccupation with "me." There are many everyday expressions of this, such as "being in someone else's shoes." The important point is to remember that they're not *your* shoes! In other words, picking up on how others might be feeling shouldn't lead to your taking on the emotion yourself. That would be sympathy. Empathy is entirely different. It is only with empathy that you can offer help with resolving their issues.

The importance of detached compassion for effective leadership was illustrated in one of our case studies, which focused on the evaluations of managers by their direct reports. Feedback on managers' performance is widely used to assess their effectiveness, and it is usually based on ratings of a series of facets of each manager's behavior. Unfortunately, the feedback systems tend to have so many different dimensions that meaningful interpretation is almost impossible. For example, the feedback system used by the large New Zealand company in which our study took place was based on 31 different dimensions, each rated on a 5-point scale. In any feedback exercise, a single manager with 30 direct reports would attract over 900 ratings! Analyzing the results of these sorts of surveys is at best messy and at worst uninterpretable, with individual managers scoring high on some measures but low on others, or with the responses of some direct reports canceling out the responses of others.

The implicit assumption is that each dimension provides an independently useful data point, but what if a subset of the measures is assessing the same thing, only in a slightly different way? One of the aims of statistics is to provide the simplest systematic but accurate way of interpreting data, and this is achieved not by the elaboration of measures but by data reduction. Applying this principle to the system used in the New Zealand company, the question was to what extent the many different dimensions could be grouped into higher-order clusters. To provide an answer, the feedback for an initial sample of managers from the company based on the 31 categories was subjected to *factor analysis*, a statistical tool that groups items together on the basis of their interrelationships, and the groupings are called *factors*. In the analysis just two main factors emerged: the first concerned *relationship skills* (including measures such as peer relationships, integrity and trust, and listening), and the second concerned *task skills* (such as measures for business acumen, action orientation, and drive for results).

For the main part of the study, a different sample of 28 middle-ranking managers was involved, each of whom had an average of

10 direct reports. Their ratings were averaged to provide a single score on each factor for each manager, and the managers' scores on each of the eight profile scales were also obtained. In addition to the eight standard scales, detached coping and sensitivity scores were pooled to provide a ninth measure of detached compassion. Statistical analysis was then used to find out which of the profile measures would predict more positive scores on the two feedback dimensions. The results showed significantly more positive feedback on relationship skills for managers who scored low on emotional inhibition and high on detached compassion. In other words, the managers who attract significantly more positive ratings are those who express emotion appropriately and can pick up quickly and accurately on how people feel without becoming identified themselves with the emotion.

When people speak to you, is your attention focused on formulating your reply?

How to change. Sensitivity is acquired by the practice of letting go of the preoccupation with "me," which allows you to see situations from others' perspective. There are many everyday expressions of this, such as being in someone else's shoes. The important point is to remember that they're not *your* shoes! In other words, picking up on how someone might be feeling shouldn't lead to your taking on the emotion yourself. That would be sympathy. Empathy is entirely different, and it is only with empathy that you can offer help with resolving their issues. A useful starting point is to notice whether or not you are actually listening when people speak to you. Is your attention on that, or are you absorbed in formulating your reply? Or worse still, are you thinking about what you have planned for the afternoon?

Try "stopping": when a colleague steps into your office to talk to you, stop whatever you are doing, so that attention is fully at your disposal. If you're at a crucial stage in a task, ask your colleague to wait until you've finished, rather than seemingly listening to him but all the while completing the task in your head. In common with all of the behaviors we're describing, sensitivity will change with practice. And don't be afraid to ask people to repeat what they've said if your attention was elsewhere. Better still, tell them you missed what they said because your attention was elsewhere—the more you can acknowledge waking sleep, the more aware of it you'll become.

Flexibility

What it looks like. Flexibility is our final index, and the title is to a large extent self-explanatory: flexible people are able to adapt more quickly and easily to change, while inflexible people dislike change and would prefer things to remain the way they are. The fact is that everything changes all the time, and having a flexible response to change is essential. The advantages of flexibility have a long history in folklore: the proud oak being dismissive of the flimsy reed until a violent gale blows the oak over; the reed flexes and survives. If you can't adapt, the consequence is much more likely to be rumination when change does happen, but there is a caveat to being flexible, and that's to be wary of loving change for its own sake.

Everything changes all the time.

How to change. Flexibility is about being able to adapt to change, and not being flexible is held in place by emotion. If you are inflexible, here's the question: what is it about change that provokes your negative emotions, especially anxiety? Most of us would prefer to know what's around the corner, but the future is unknown. If you think that changes being proposed at work are not useful, you should say so, but only after letting go of any negative emotions the proposals have provoked. Most of us can recall angrily protesting about something, which probably led to others' taking up the opposite position equally strongly.

It is just as important to let go of your negative responses if the changes are implemented anyway. There's nothing worse than listening to someone going on and on about how much better things were at some time in the past. When we dislike change, our recollections of how things were before are almost always rose tinted. If there isn't anything you can do about the changes that are made, there are two appropriate responses: accept and embrace the changes, which will give you the opportunity to be instrumental in them, or leave.

The other side of the coin is making changes when they're not actually necessary. This is especially true for people in management roles, where moving the goalposts all the time will inevitably make your team feel anxious and uncertain. Restructuring is an important part of adapting to change, but it needs to be done strategically, when it is actually required. When a new team leader is appointed, he or she will bring a different perspective. These new ideas might well be of enormous benefit, but the benefit needs to be measured against the desire simply to make one's mark, imposing one's preferences on the team, whether or not the changes are useful. If you're in this position, before going full-steam ahead, first decide, in as detached a frame of mind as possible, whether the changes you want to make will really be helpful. Take the time to consult with team members: What is it that they feel ought to change? What works well and is best left in place? A more dangerous motive for change is boredom. Wanting stimulation for its own sake or impulsiveness must be kept in check if an organization is to succeed.

THE RELATIONSHIPS AMONG THE DIMENSIONS

We're often asked how the different scales are related to one another. There are some relationships, but they're not straightforward. For example, rumination and emotional inhibition are completely unrelated. Statistically, their correlation is around zero, and what that means is that you can have any pattern of scores: high on both, low on both, or low on one but high on the other. At the other extreme is the rumination and detached coping pair, which correlate highly inversely—statistically, if you have a high score on one, you're likely to have a low score on the other. The less you're able to keep perspective and the more you tend to catastrophize issues, the more likely you are to ruminate about them.

The problem, though, is that if you run a matrix of correlations among almost any collection of behavioral measures, you're likely to find some correlations, but that doesn't mean that any two that do correlate are measuring the same thing. Without digressing too far into statistics, you could represent the two behavioral domains as circles. If you had a perfect positive correlation (+1.00), you could then confidently say that they are measuring the same thing, and the two circles would overlap completely. If there were no correlation between them (a correlation coefficient of zero), the two circles would not overlap at all. You can estimate the size of the overlap by squaring the coefficient and multiplying by 100, which gives you an estimate of the percentage of what's called the *shared variance* between them. In the case of rumination and detached coping, the correlation is around –0.80 (the minus indicates that they're inversely correlated, meaning the higher the score on one, the lower the score is likely to be on the other), so we'd get a figure of 64. This tells us that the circles overlap 64 percent. A correlation of this magnitude is high, but it is far from a complete overlap; in fact, there is 36 percent of the variance that they don't share.

Applying this to the research findings, depending on what you're investigating, sometimes rumination will be the significant factor, and in other cases detached coping will be. Using two measures simultaneously will often provide a more powerful predictor than either separately. For example, measuring the effects of rumination and emotional inhibition on physiological recovery after exposure to laboratory stress, rumination significantly predicts delayed recovery. Emotional inhibition also predicts slower recovery, but less significantly. However, when you select people who score high on both scales, they take the longest to recover of all three groups.

Emotional inhibition/rumination is the least related pair among the eight scales, while detached coping/rumination represents the most related pair. Correlations among the remaining scales tend to show coefficients similar to those found with any set of individual differences, around the 0.20 to 0.30 mark, though another problem with correlation coefficients is that how significant they are depends on the size of the sample—the larger the sample, the smaller it needs to be for it to be significant. So with a large enough sample, 0.30 might be significant, even though the two circles actually only overlap 9 percent. What we also need to bear in mind is that a correlation isn't a causal relationship. We can't conclude from the correlation between rumination and detached coping that the one causes the other. All we know is that they're associated.

ANOTHER DIMENSION: MEDITATION

We made a link earlier in the book between resilience and mindfulness. Unfortunately, "mindfulness" has become just another bit of psychobabble, but the link can be made simply and clearly by asking, what is your mind full of?

Unless you're in deep sleep, it might be dreams in dreaming sleep or waking sleep, or it might be nightmares while you're physically asleep or when you're ruminating. There is a third option: when the dreams and nightmares are let go, what's left filling the mind is attention, not attached to anything in particular. It then becomes a powerful tool, allowing you to intentionally focus it, to use the past and the future to draw on experience and formulate plans but keeping the present as the frame of reference.

Mindfulness, in turn, is linked to meditation. The word *meditation* often evokes ideas that tie it to one or another spiritual tradition. This can deter people from inquiring any further, which is unfortunate. The benefits of meditation are well documented. Innumerable studies of its effects have shown significant benefits for health and well-being. The good news is that meditation practice is becoming much more acceptable. Meditation is an extremely simple and direct practice of Challenge of Change Resilience Training: being fully awake, with attention controlled and completely focused. Meditation helps to establish mindfulness, making you less subject to the antics of a mind that is always elsewhere, but we need to place it firmly in the realm of our everyday life.

You don't need to sit in a lotus position. A comfortable chair works fine, provided that you're not so comfortable, you drift into sleep! It is best not to lie down, mainly because during meditation your body will be relaxed, and by a simple association, being relaxed and lying down will often lead to sleep. Meditation isn't sleeping, though even experienced meditators will sometimes nod off. All that means is that you're tired and you need to rest, so if you're trying to meditate but you just keep nodding off, have a nap and return to it later.

There isn't a fixed time in the day for meditating or a fixed length of time to meditate. We tend to be more wakeful in the morning, and morning and evening are propitious to the extent that we've not yet started work or have finished for the day, but that's all. Since it takes a while for your mind to settle, half an hour seems about right, but when you first begin, that can feel like an awfully long time. There's no point in forcing it, so when you start, a useful strategy is to set an alarm for maybe 10 minutes. When it rings, if all you've been doing is struggling to still your mind, stop and try again the next day. You should find that gradually you're comfortable to continue after the alarm has sounded, so just continue until it feels natural to stop.

Make sure you won't be interrupted. Once you've found a comfortable position in the chair, place your feet flat on the floor. Crossed legs will tend to inhibit blood circulation, and you'll need to move around sooner. Having your arms folded is also usually less comfortable, so try with your hands loose in your lap. You're going to close your eyes next, so look around before you begin so that you're not distracted by wondering about your surroundings, especially if you're sitting outside.

Once you feel comfortable, close your eyes. Control your attention by giving it intentionally to physical sensations: the weight of your body in the chair, the pressure of your clothes against your skin. Then attend to your breathing—take a deep breath first if you feel that you need to, and then relax your chest and stomach, allowing each breath to come and go without any effort. A lot of tension collects around the point where your neck and shoulders meet. You can think of this as a kind of gate that becomes tightly shut when you're tense, so just let all of that tension go by relaxing your arms and your hands, and then your neck, your scalp, and your face. Let all tension go from around your eyes, your mouth, and your jaw, and with each out breath, let go of any remaining physical tension. Another gate is located in your pelvis. Relax the muscles in your stomach, and extend that to your legs and feet. Feel the weight of your feet on the floor, and keep releasing tension with each out breath. Sometimes people try to relax by progressively tensing up muscle groups and then relaxing them, but you're introducing tension where there might be none at all, and with short muscle groups like your hands and forearms, the tension can then be even harder to release.

So far, this is relaxation, and even this practice on its own can be very useful. To really have an effect, you need to relax your mind, which is what meditation is. A helpful way to start is to be aware of any sounds you can hear. The sounds are associated with particular things, and they will usually bring a picture of it to mind, or some sounds might feel like an irritating distraction. These conditioned responses are to be expected, but they can easily be elaborated on, and we end up just thinking instead of meditating. This is why we need something to focus our attention, perhaps a word that you repeat in your mind, which is called a *mantra*. Much is said about mantras and how they have special powers, but in fact you can use any word at all: "sock" will do, even "butter." Mantras are often Sanskrit words or phrases, and it can be helpful if you don't know the language because there will be fewer associations. All you need to do is repeat the word in your mind. What it does is give you something to focus attention on, so when it gets distracted, you can bring it back to focus on the word and away from your thoughts.

Many people find it much easier to focus on breathing, using the cool sensation in your nose as you breathe in and the warm sensation as you breathe out as the focus for attention. Whether it is a word or your breathing, your mind will pretty quickly decide it's boring and will go off in search of something else, like the report you have to write or what you're planning for the weekend. Don't be disheartened. This is exactly what you can expect: your mind wanting stimulation and wandering off. Just bring your attention back each time it does, and your mind will gradually settle. You can meditate with your eyes open and focused on a particular object—a flower, for example. With your eyes open, there is much more that you're aware of, so it is a more difficult practice, but the process is the same, bringing attention back each time to the object until your mind stops rebelling.

In principle, this is all that meditation is: sitting still, controlling your attention, and letting go of distractions.

In principle, this is all that meditation is: sitting still, controlling and focusing your attention, and letting go of distractions. With practice it can deepen, to the point where the awareness of the repeated word or breathing fade as well, and there is really nothing on your mind. However deep it is, though, any practice of really letting go like this will have a significant effect, enabling you to wake up more consistently, to control your attention more effectively, to keep things more in perspective, and to let go far more easily of emotional attachments. Try it!

A WIDER PERSPECTIVE: RESILIENCE AND WELL-BEING

An important reason for increasing resilience skills is the effect it has on well-being. Most people have an intuitive sense of what *well-being* means, but like *happiness*, it can be an overinclusive generalization. At the broadest level, well-being is both physical and mental. Just as body and mind can't easily be separated, the two are interdependent: mental well-being is signaled by happiness, but being physically well is a key component of that. Strategies for increasing well-being were at one time regarded with a great deal of skepticism, but mindfulness, fitness, nutrition, meditation, yoga, massage, and the like are increasingly being introduced directly into organizations.

Feedback indicates that employees have a very positive view of strategies to increase well-being, but untangling the myths from real evidence of their benefits is difficult. This is especially true for diet—despite claims made by manufacturers of supplements, controlled trials testing their effectiveness generally reveal more quackery and marketing hype than actual benefits. Our physiological systems operate in highly complex, interactive ways that don't reflect the simplistic idea that if something is good for you, the more you have of it, the healthier you'll be. Properly controlled trials of vitamin supplements show none of the claimed effects on memory, cancer, or heart disease. Our bodies are based on homeostatic principles, and when the required level of most vitamins is reached, the rest is dispensed with. Unless you have a particular medical problem, if you follow straightforward advice about ensuring a balanced diet, you have no need for supplements; all that you create by taking them is very expensive urine.

One thing is certain: unless you're clinically depressed and need medication to treat it, there is no pill in the world that will keep you happier or less stressed. Any benefits from taking psychoactive "happy pills" will be temporary. If you want real well-being, you need to get to the heart of it, which is the way you think. Consider this: your body is a completely inert, biochemically self-regulating system. What upsets that system is thoughts. Try the exercise we suggested for toxic achievers, using an electronic blood-pressure monitor. Take a measure while you're just listening to sounds around you, without imagining any stories about what you hear. Connect with your sense of sound, and take a measure. Next think about something pleasant you enjoy doing, not exciting, just enjoyable, and take a measure. Now think about something that really upsets you: the argument you had with your manager or your partner, or the state you were in after you'd been publicly criticized, and take a third measure. There'll likely be little difference between the first two, but the third will be significantly higher, purely as a result of ruminating about emotional upset. Stress really is all in the mind.

It is widely assumed that stress plays an important role in cancer, but cancer is not *caused* by stress—it is primarily a genetic disease, and what your body does bring to the party is DNA. Whether or not you develop an illness like cancer is likely to be an interaction between your genetic predispositions, random changes in your genes, and what you're exposed to. What habitual rumination will do is sustain elevations in cortisol secretion, which might in turn affect the spread of cancer by compromising immunity—stress does appear to reduce survival rates in cancer patients. In the same way, sustained elevations in adrenaline impose cardiac strain, and the link to heart disease is probably more direct than it is with cancer, but the complex interaction with genetics, diet, and exercise mean that the link is again not straightforward. Over the last century life expectancy has steadily increased in the Western world, but it would be a mistake to want to develop resilience just in order to live longer. If you are more resilient, you may well do so, and maintaining good health does contribute to well-being, but it isn't the quantity of life that's important but the quality of it.

Exercise is thought to combat stress. Unlike dietary fads, the health benefits of exercise are real and demonstrable. There is a wealth of expensive equipment available, but all you need is a good pair of walking boots or decent sneakers. Although regular exercise does contribute significantly to physical health, it is not in itself a way to reduce stress. People sometimes say that when they get stressed out, all they need to do is go for a 10-mile run. The question is, what does your mind do while you are running? If the answer is ruminate, you'll end up fit and miserable. The best way to think about stress and exercise is to go back to controlling attention. If instead of ruminating on your run, you use the opportunity to reflect on issues in a detached way, or better still, connect your attention with the world around you, there's no processing room left for rumination. By the end of the run, reflection might well have provided the perspective needed to resolve an issue.

The key to incorporating diet and exercise into a well-being routine is balance. Unfortunately, in the context of stress and resilience, it is most often expressed as "work-life balance," which implies that at work you don't have a life! These sorts of ideas feed into the perception of work as something that has to be endured and escaped from at every opportunity, and all that does is to make work a chore. There is a balance to be struck, but getting the right balance applies to pretty much everything we do. Once you divide the world up into what you love to do and what you hate to do, you're bound to wish that the former will pass quickly and the latter go on for as long as possible. Nothing lasts, so taking this view will inevitably leave you dissatisfied: unhappy at the start of what you hate, and unhappy when what you love comes to an end.

When it comes to steps you can take in the wider context of health and resilience, our advice would be to proceed with caution. Arranging one-off half-marathons for staff is not a good idea, unless you can ensure that they're fit enough to do it. One large team we work with thought carefully about what would work best. They have a masseuse who visits one day a week, going from desk to desk assessing posture and offering advice as well as massage. They have a nutritionist who comes once a month, and team members schedule appointments through the day. They subsidize gym memberships, and they offer guided mindfulness practice after work for those who are interested (about half the team, as it happens). Those who want additional consultations with experts can do so privately if they find the services helpful. The system was trialed for a six-month period, and coupled with the resilience training, the effects were so marked that the system has become a permanent fixture. This is the way to proceed, with evidence to back up the strategies you decide to introduce.

PERSONALITY AND LEADERSHIP

In the workshops we run, all participants complete the same profile, whether they are leaders or team members, but the implications of their individual profiles are different: a toxic team member is much more easily dealt with than having the team led by a confirmed toxic achiever. Unfortunately, there are companies where this kind of behavior is admired, and it can become the culture of the organization; thankfully, they seem to be the minority. As we noted earlier, levels of reported stress do seem to diminish the higher you go in an organization. A likely reason is that in mindful organizations, people are promoted for the right reason: they're more resilient because they've learned the skills themselves. In fact, many of the leaders in our programs comment that at the start of their careers, their rumination and other scores would have been much worse, but over time, they learned to do many of the things outlined in this book.

The problem is that this learning has been a haphazard process of trial and error, and an equal number express regret that no one taught them all of this at the beginning of their careers! This is a view echoed across all levels in our training. The good news is that it's never too late to become more resilient, but it is especially important for those nearer the start of their careers. The eight dimensions from the Challenge of Change Resilience Profile that we've described in this chapter provide a clear, evidence-based overview of what it takes to stay resilient under pressure, how to identify what your strengths and weaknesses are, and what you need to start doing to shorten the learning process to becoming resilient. Here's what the difference looks like between leaders who have skilled, highly resilient profiles and those who do not:

Skilled in Resilience

- Express appropriately how they are feeling about things

- Keep a healthy balance between *what* goals are achieved and *how* they are achieved

- Have high standards, but don't try to perfect what is already fit for its purpose

- Address concerns they have quickly rather than letting them fester

- Can walk into a meeting and pick up quickly on the emotional tone in the room and how individuals are feeling

- Are sensitive to others' emotions, while staying detached enough not to take on these emotions

- Adapt quickly to organizational changes and look to make the most of the new reality

Unskilled in Resilience

- Ruminate about most areas of their life, both personal and professional

- Tend to bottle up emotions rather than sharing them, and tend to regard expressing emotion as a weakness

- Often make it hard for others to read what they are thinking or feeling about a situation

- Want work done yesterday and become hostile and angry when they don't get their way

- Fail to see the diminishing returns from continuing to polish a piece of work

- Avoid speaking directly to people who have upset them

- Are either highly sensitive and can't detach (hypersensitive) or are highly detached with little sensitivity (aloof)

We can't emphasize enough that the attitudes and behaviors in our eight measures are changeable, so here are four steps you can take as a leader to help effect the changes needed in yourself:

1. Find a rumination partner. While some appreciate the positive impact of expressing their emotions, they are not sure how best to begin. Two people we worked with decided to become rumination partners: if either one of them found that he was ruminating, he could go to the partner's office and vent for five minutes. The rules were that the partner wasn't allowed to try to solve the problem, give advice, or get involved, and it worked perfectly. What they created was a safe, private, and nonjudgmental environment in which to speak openly about how they felt, and it left both of them feeling much better and less burdened. So think about it, and act on it: who would be a good rumination partner for you?

2. Beware of overused strengths. When leaders learn about their profile, many are pleased to see themselves being well in the right direction on some of the scales. We caution them, however, that any strength that is used to excess can become a weakness. Leaders who score high in *flexibility*, for example, are generally resilient during times of change because they adapt to what the new change brings. Some leaders are so comfortable with change that they make changes constantly, without appreciating that change may not be necessary and that not everyone on their team would score high on flexibility. Similarly, being low on avoidance coping is advantageous. These leaders confront issues that are on their minds rather than pushing them to one side, but taken too far, they can end up evoking a response (usually unspoken!) along the lines of, "What, you want to give me *more* feedback?"

3. Find your opposite thinker. One of the challenges of changing our thinking is that most of us believe that ours is the natural and correct way to think and act and that others think as we do (or if they don't, they just don't get it!). It isn't until you start sharing your results with those at the other end of the profile spectrum that you start to see that yours is just one view. A good example that often comes up in the training is people who score high on rumination—they really believe that's the way they are and that it is impossible not to ruminate, especially given all the organizational changes and uncertainty that might be going on. When we suggest that it is indeed possible, they often push back and say we couldn't possibly understand what they're facing. We then facilitate conversations between them and resilient colleagues who are involved in the same circumstances but who don't ruminate. What they say about the way they're responding without stress directly challenges the assumption that stress is inevitable. Seeing that it is possible not to get stressed then opens people's minds to learning about how to do it.

4. Master the two Rs of leadership. When Peter Friedes became CEO of Hewitt Associates, he noticed that his top leaders all shared two common features.

First, they all had *relationship* skills: they asked their people questions, and they listened to and supported their teams. But this alone was not enough since some average leaders also did those things.

To be a truly outstanding leader, his top leaders also had a second R: *requiring* skills. Leaders who were skilled at requiring set high standards, encouraged people to achieve, and held people accountable. Friedes noticed that some leaders were good at relating, others were good at requiring, but it was the leaders who practiced doing both that achieved outstanding results. These were the leaders who required (and got) high performance without alienating their people, which is exactly what we found in our case study of leaders with detached compassion.

Look at your own leadership style, and notice if you are more comfortable relating (linked to sensitivity and emotional expression) or more comfortable requiring (linked to detachment). This will tell you if you are neglecting one side or the other. Remember, the best bosses consistently push people to do their best and offer high doses of support. It is not a complicated formula. It's just not that commonly applied.

SUMMARY

- *Personality* is often thought to describe characteristics and behaviors that are hardwired and unchangeable. We use the word to describe habitual behaviors acquired primarily by conditioning, which can be changed with training.

- Of the eight psychometric measures of resilience that we've developed, rumination is the most important, and detached coping is the second most important.

- The remaining scales, which all contribute to being more or less resilient, are emotional inhibition, toxic achieving, avoidance coping, perfect control, sensitivity, and flexibility.

- The relationships among the scales vary from being completely independent (rumination and emotional inhibition) to being moderately highly correlated (rumination and detached coping), but they all measure unique facets of resilience.

- The two measures detached coping and sensitivity can be combined to provide a measure of empathy that is significantly related to more positive ratings of managers by their direct reports.

- Resilient leaders:

  - Find a rumination partner.

  - Do not overuse strengths.

  - Find opposite thinkers.

  - Master the two Rs of leadership—relating and requiring.

6

RESILIENT COMMUNICATION AND LEADING CHANGE

This chapter represents a shift from discussing the personal aspects of resilience to focusing on the interpersonal ones. We will not be digressing into a review of communication skills training, other than to provide a context for exploring how we can apply the same four steps of waking up, controlling attention, becoming detached, and letting go to developing more effective ways to communicate. A key element in facilitating change is being able to communicate effectively, and good communication is especially important in avoiding misunderstandings between managers and their teams. These communication techniques will enable managers to begin to behave more like leaders.

COMMUNICATION SKILLS:
AN ALTERNATIVE APPROACH

Our interest in communication arose from a series of resilience training sessions we were running in a large U.K. company. Staff in the company was asked to complete an annual engagement survey, and although the results suggested that the overall climate in the company was good, it was patchy. There was a wide variation across teams, and the main contributor to low engagement seemed mainly to do with poor communication. Staff also uniformly reported that poor communication was contributing significantly to their feeling stressed as well as disengaged. Communication skills training was available for staff in the company, but it didn't appear to be having any tangible effect, so we decided to include in the resilience program many of the communications skills we discuss in this chapter.

Staff uniformly reported that poor communication was contributing significantly to their feeling stressed.

One way is to improve eye contact. When someone you're talking to steadfastly looks over your shoulder, it can be very disconcerting, and the opposite may be true too: unwavering eye contact can make the conversation seem more like an interrogation. Maintaining appropriate eye contact is undoubtedly important, and a rule that is sometimes suggested is that it should be about 50 percent of the time. However, patterns of eye contact are highly variable, depending on factors such as how formal the conversation is or the complexity of the information being conveyed. When someone is reflecting on a proposal you're suggesting, especially a complex one, he will often break eye contact, not because he has lost interest but because it is easier for him to reflect if he is not focused on you. Skilled communicators might use a wide range of eye-contact patterns within the same conversation.

Another feature of good communication skills is the ability to listen. This might seem obvious, yet most people have had the experience of talking to someone and seeing the blinds come down—the lights are on, but there's no one home! Another way of thinking about this is attention control: when the blinds come down, attention has been pulled away to something else. However, this may be because your listener is reflecting on what you've said. She is going into the past or the future intentionally to make sense of the problem. The simple solution is to wait or to check whether clarification is needed.

Then again your listener might have drifted into waking sleep. We all know that feeling of having heard it all before, and instead of listening, whatever we're going to do next weekend becomes a lot more interesting. Worse still, if we're being criticized, we might add negative emotion to the daydream and turn it into a nightmare of rumination. When attention is drawn away into waking sleep or rumination, your listener is effectively no longer there and you might as well talk to the wall.

Figure 6.1 is the same diagram we used in Chapter 2 (Figure 2.2) to show the changing states of waking and sleeping. In which of these states are you actually available and able to communicate? It has to be only when you're awake. The first two steps in our system apply equally to communication: to do so effectively, you have to be awake and controlling your attention. Controlled attention means giving it to the here and now—in other words, listening to what is being said. Communication is disrupted by interference, which can take external or internal forms. An example of *external disruption* is when you're speaking and someone interrupts you;

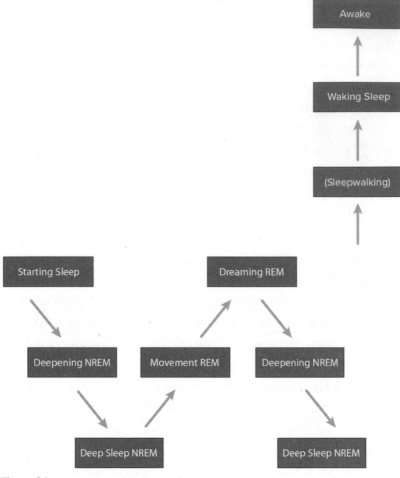

Figure 6.1

internal disruption is losing attention control and drifting into waking sleep or rumination.

Communication is much more likely to provoke rumination when it involves a personal attack on someone, so another principle of communicating more effectively is *to make it as impersonal as possible*. Suppose you spend a lot of time preparing a project report, but it doesn't meet the required standard. At the meeting, your manager has two broad options for telling you this: he can say either (1) that the *work* you submitted hasn't reached the required standard or (2) that *you* have failed to reach the required standard.

Another principle of communicating more effectively is to make it as impersonal as possible.

The difference might seem trivial, until you consider the consequences. In the first option there is an acknowledgment that the work hasn't met expectations, and the opportunity is available for your manager to find out whether you might need more help or further training in the required skills, or perhaps more experience at preparing project reports. In the second option you are personally blamed for the shortcoming in the work, which will inevitably provoke some combination of guilt, embarrassment, and anger, especially if the comments are made in front of colleagues. You might still do what's needed, but it is very likely to be compromised because it is accompanied by rumination.

DEPERSONALIZING COMMUNICATION

Let's suppose I work for you, in which case there are three elements in our relationship: you, me, and the work. In one possible scenario, I'm attached to the work that I do, so we could place me and my work on one side. On the other side is you. In this scenario there is a legitimate target, the work. You're my manager, and part of your role is to evaluate what I do. However, if my work and I are merged, then whatever you say about the work not being up to snuff will apply to me as well. Your job is to evaluate what I do, but you've ended up also evaluating me, and that isn't your role. My work needs to reach a certain standard, but I don't—whatever you might think of me personally is not a factor. So there are two potential mistakes involved here: as my manager, you are using the shortcoming in my work to blame me, or I may assume that whatever you're saying about my work also applies to me, even if that isn't your intention. Worst of all, you might be intending to apportion blame while I'm actively taking it on.

In a second possible scenario, you and I are on the same side, and the work is on the other. What has happened is that I've become detached from the work and can let go of the personalizing that goes with thinking I am my job. You might say that this is letting go of ownership and responsibility, but the problem is with the language: responsibility carries an explicit sense of identification and blame. We certainly have tasks we're required to fulfill, and we do them to the best of our abilities and within the constraints of time and money. Words such as *ownership* and *responsibility* are loaded with the potential for feeling failure and being blamed. Why do we feel we need to hold the sword of Damocles over people who are doing their best to achieve the goals we've set them? And why do we assume that if we don't imply blame, we'll be allowing others to get away with anything they like?

When people are given a task, there is an expectation that they'll deliver. If they don't, there is a reason for it—most people don't intentionally do a bad job. In fact, one of the criteria for being a leader instead of a manager is to assume that everyone wants to do the best they can. Let's take fault out of it altogether. If something doesn't work out as planned, what can we—together, on the same side—do to try to ensure that it works out better next time? Before you engage in a blaming exercise, try asking yourself whether *you've* always done everything to perfection, and work from there. A blaming culture is informed by a fundamental belief that threat and blame get things done. As with toxic achieving managers, the job may get done, but at a significant cost to teamwork and loyalty.

A phrase that is commonly used to mask blame is *constructive criticism*, but criticism is never constructive. The phrase is a contradiction: *constructing* is putting together, while *criticism* is taking apart. Most people who have been on the receiving end of so-called constructive criticism will probably tell you they felt taken apart, and as a consequence, they ruminated about it afterward. People will often defend constructive criticism as a means for people to learn from their mistakes, but when you explore this further, it is apparent that there's an implicit assumption that people feel guilty, so they won't do it again, supposedly learning from guilt. Feeling guilty is a useless waste of attention. When you see that what you've done doesn't reach the required standard, learning about it happens right then and there. Guilt is just a form of rumination. And what's a mistake? A lack of practiced skill. How long did it take *you* to acquire the skills to be expert at what you do?

The negative effects of criticism might be unintentional, but saying you didn't mean to have that effect doesn't prevent it from happening. Communication needs to be mindful, so that you're aware of the effects of what comes out of your mouth. This is one of the key differences between managers and leaders. Much of what passes for management training is about process, which is important, but anyone can do process. Leadership is quite different. People follow managers because they have to; they follow leaders because they want to. You don't respect those whose default mode is criticism.

*People follow managers because they have to;
they follow leaders because they want to.*

The principle of separating the person from the work is implicit in child-rearing. When children step out of line and misbehave, what do you comment on, the behavior or the child? Always the behavior, not the child. The appropriate response isn't, "You idiot, what did you do that for?" but rather, "If you behave like that, it will upset people, so try not to do it again." Criticism destroys self-esteem and turns people against you, which we know when we deal with our children. Why is it thrown out the window when we're dealing with adults?

Behavior here is not what the child is but what he does, and that tacit assumption extends to our attitudes. If a member of your team has an attitude problem that's affecting everyone else, take the person aside—this is always done privately—and point out that he has a way of *behaving* (acting or speaking) that is causing problems for the team. Reassure him that it is just a habit that he may not even be aware of, but it does need to change. Describe it as precisely as you can, and then give him the opportunity to change, with the further reassurance that if he finds it difficult, you can arrange for some individual mentoring for him. An important qualification is not to expect change overnight. A caveat: There are those who habitually take things personally. If they are on your team, use extra care when dealing with them. A feature of good leadership is not assuming that one style fits all—people are individuals, and they have to be dealt with accordingly. Learning to be resilient can go a long way toward addressing people's self-perceptions, and the training program is in part about enhancing self-esteem. But when dealing with those who find it difficult to change, your expectations need to be realistic.

The effects of habitual attitudes and behavior are even more important for managers because the way they act will directly affect all of the members of their teams. Based on the resilience training, there are specific steps that can be taken to address management style and to transform mere managers into leaders.

LEADING CHANGE

The two interrelated conditions under which people in organizations are more likely to ruminate are high uncertainty and a perceived lack of control. Because both conditions are common during times of large-scale change, it is important that leaders communicate in a way that reduces rather than fuels these conditions. Leaders themselves are usually experiencing the same challenges as their people, so they need to be particularly mindful not just of the words they use but also their body language and tone of voice: they may be communicating more than they think. The way we communicate becomes so automated and habitual that we may not be aware of what skilled communication looks like, but it can be systematically described:

Leaders Skilled in Communicating

- Consult those who will have to implement the change early to get their input

- Tell people what is currently known about the change and what is currently unknown

- Adjust communication style and level of detail to the needs of their audience

- Give people honest and clear feedback about their behaviors and their impact

- Help people make sense of what the change will mean to them

- Help direct reports work out what they can stop doing, not just what they need to add

- Hold frequent milestone meetings to focus on the change through to completion

Leaders Unskilled in Communicating

- Pass on information about the change from above, but don't translate what that means at different levels

- Rush the implementation of the change without paying attention to people's reactions to it

- Make decisions that will affect the implementers without getting input and buy-in from them first

- Deliver feedback that focuses on the person rather than the work

- Talk constantly about the change, but not about everything that is staying constant

- Overfocus on the needs of the team, while neglecting to look after themselves

The key to being a true leader is not just being able to drive for results. Working effectively with people is as much about how well you can communicate, and people skills are a significant part of what makes the difference. People will follow leaders willingly because they respect them, and that respect comes primarily from their people skills. The term *business acumen* is widely used and is generally assumed to be about financial literacy. One of the Challenge of Change Resilience Training providers in New Zealand, Cynthia Johnson, decided to dig a little deeper by conducting detailed interviews with successful CEOs. Factor analyzing their responses yielded a clear structure that included financial literacy but as only one factor; the other two were passion for the job and having people skills.

Teams generally have a structure that can be expressed in a tree diagram, with diminishing authority as you move lower down the tree and with clear labels for each level and each role. For example, a sales team might have a single senior sales manager at the top, with the next level having perhaps five managers each responsible for different sales areas across the country. They will in turn have salespeople reporting to them, each responsible for a different geographic area, as well as various administrative staff. The tree is the formal organization, and it describes how the different roles relate to one another and what their levels of status or influence are. Unfortunately, what the diagram doesn't show is the *informal* structure: who gets along with whom, which people or teams are competing with one another, how effective each of the managers is, and so on. A significant determinant of informal structure is the behavior of team leaders. Here are some specific strategies that can be used to improve leaders' communication skills.

1. Communicate the four Ps of the change. When a change happens in an organization, people can struggle to make sense of what it means for them. If a leader can help them do this quickly and efficiently, the team can avoid hours, days, or weeks of ruminative thinking. William Bridges, a leading researcher on change, points out that there are 4 Ps that people want to know during any change:

> *Purpose.* "Why are we making this change? What is the rationale behind it?"

> *Picture.* "What is the end state we are trying to get to?"

Plan. "What are the steps we need to take to get there?"

Part. "What is my role in the change? How do I help?"

Leaders who fail to answer these questions for their people leave a vacuum of uncertainty, which often is filled with rumination. Whenever you are leading a change, begin by communicating with your people about what the four Ps are for this change and for them.

2. Talk more about what is *not* changing. During new organizational initiatives, leaders often are told that they should be communicating constantly about the change. While this initially sounds right, our experience is that it often leads to unnecessary anxiety as people come to believe that more is changing in the organization than really is. The fact is that during most change initiatives, the majority of things will stay exactly the same: you will work at the same desk, sit with the same people, and use the same computer to do the same job.

The paradox for the leader is that the bigger the change, the more you have to emphasize what is *stable*. When Nelson Mandela led South Africa through the end of apartheid, the greatest challenge he faced wasn't getting the change to happen but creating enough stability that the nation didn't shatter. So when you are leading change, give as much emphasis to what is staying the same as to what is changing.

3. Identify the organization's change equation. Researchers who study change estimate that as much as 70 percent of all change efforts fail to achieve what they set out to do. Given the significant amount of time, money, and effort wasted on these failures, you'd think that organizations would be analyzing their data to find out what distinguishes the successful change initiatives from the failures, but most organizations are simply too busy to take the time to do the analyses.

To help resolve the problem, we initiated a research project to help organizations do just that. Our research showed that there was no generic set of factors that applied to all organizations: organizational cultures vary so much that what leads to success at one company might get you fired at another. In some cases change is more successful when leaders are consultative, in others when they're more directive, and in others still when it is less about the leaders and more about the people who will enact the change. Unless you can systematically unpack how your organization really works, it can be difficult to craft a change strategy. To find out more about what your organization's *change equation* might look like, visit http://bit.ly/1OlH1wh.

4. Beware of the weeds. Recently we were working with a team from an engineering company who were particularly skilled at finding problems and trying to solve them. This made them good at their jobs, but it was problematic in meetings because every time someone mentioned a challenge, everyone would dive straight into the details and start trying to solve it immediately. The effect was that they often got lost in the weeds. After watching them get stuck several times, we pointed this out to them. They recognized it as a habit they had and wondered what sort of training they would need to overcome it. "No training needed," we replied, "just call 'Weeds.' The problem is not that you don't know how to pull yourself out of it. Your problem is that you don't alert each other quickly enough when you are doing it. The next time someone on the team spots that you're getting stuck in the details, just call out, 'Weeds.'"

Over the next two days whenever a team member called "Weeds," everyone would laugh, nod, and refocus on the bigger picture.

All teams have habits that they fall into, which often have to do with their professional training. Leaders must point this out to their teams and have a word or phrase to remind them, "We are doing it again." What are the habits that you notice in your team or company culture that need to be called out?

5. Acknowledge self-motivation: an antidote to micromanaging.
Managers sometimes complain that one or more of their staff is not sufficiently motivated. People do make wrong decisions about their careers, they end up in jobs they're no longer passionate about, or they have too large a workload and feel unsupported. Instead of complaining about the lack of motivation, find out why. The first principle here is to assume that everyone wants to do his or her best. If that's the case, what's become the obstacle to that happening?

If you respect your people and they respect you, then when you arrange to meet a team member to find out why she seems to have gone off the rails, the conversation will not be predicated on blame but rather a genuine effort to help, both for her benefit and that of the team. You might discover she is having a hard time personally. Since it has nothing to do directly with work, it might not be your business, but the effects of rumination are seldom compartmentalized. They leak into work from home and from home to work, so offering avenues to help is in everyone's interests. Maybe this person isn't actually able to do the job she has been given, but she has been reluctant to acknowledge it. In which case, arrange for specific practical help, such as more training.

Perhaps this person has just ended up in the wrong place and needs a change. You can try to find a more appropriate position for her in the company, though it might also be that the time has come for her to move on. A manager in one company we worked with had joined in the role of an archivist, but he had become a manager, which he definitely didn't want to do. He listened very attentively during the Challenge of Change Resilience Training program. A week later, he submitted his resignation. When asked why, he said it was because of the program—it had given him the courage to make the move. Prior to that, each time he thought about moving, he catastrophized everything, imagining himself jobless, impoverished, and begging on the streets—the worst things in our lives that generally don't happen.

He worked for an enlightened organization that recognized that he no longer fit the role, and they actively helped him make the transition. We were working for the same company a while later, and he called to say that he had found a job running an antiquarian bookshop, which he loved. He'd taken a pay cut, but he and his family were happy once again. You can't buy happiness, and no amount of misery is worth putting up with for the sake of the money. It goes without saying that a drastic move should be based on a strategic plan and not just a whim, and there are not always jobs available that you can shift to, but the major obstacle to change is fear. The reason you're unhappy might also be because you're a professional ruminator, and since you take your mind with you wherever you go, you might be just as unhappy in the new job—not because of the job but because of your habitual tendency to ruminate!

Assuming that people want to do the best they can is also a powerful antidote to micromanagement. The reason to micromanage is that these managers don't trust their team. Managers have to set the strategies and the goals very clearly, but after that, they need to get out of the way and become interested bystanders— monitor progress, be available to provide help, but intervene only when necessary. In fact, if your people trust you, they won't go on pretending they're coping with the job, and they will let you know when they need help. And when you have to intervene, do so from the perspective of detached compassion, which allows an objective evaluation of the way people set about solving problems. There are many routes to the same outcome, but micromanagers think there's just one right way—theirs!

6. Become counselors. To become effective leaders, managers should be counselors. What this doesn't mean is having an open door for people to talk endlessly about their personal problems. If someone is struggling with personal issues, he may well need professional counseling. Instead, we're using the term *counseling* generically. A team is not a homogeneous entity but a collection of often very different people. Managers need to acquire the skills that counselors employ.

We know from our own research that real people skills include the appropriate expression of emotion and cultivating detached compassion, both cornerstones of resilient leadership. Empathize with the problems people encounter without becoming personally involved. Counseling is also a private matter, so when mistakes need correcting, always do so privately. Ask yourself whether you've ever failed to deliver—even with the best of intentions, sometimes we just run out of time or resources.

7. Avoid giving team members things to ruminate about. Criticism is almost always perceived as an attack on our self-esteem, and the consequence of criticism will inevitably be rumination by the person on the receiving end. Criticism is never constructive, so avoid giving people things to ruminate about.

There was a performance issue with a member of one of the teams we were working with. The team leader happened to be rushing between meetings when he bumped into this person. All he said was, "There's some good news and some bad news!" and he went off to his next meeting. The team member had a tendency to ruminate anyway, and all he reported doing for the next week until he could get clarification was to ruminate endlessly about what the bad news might be. This was a consequence of mindless (as opposed to mindful) communication.

As it happens this team leader wasn't a particularly poor manager, but he had a strong tendency toward impulsive extraversion. Impulsive extraverts tend to speak before they've engaged their minds. Giving his team member something to ruminate about was an inadvertent consequence of this particular manager's personality. However, it shouldn't be taken as an excuse. Even though extraversion has a significant genetic component, extraverts are nonetheless able to act more mindfully. Speech is preceded by thoughts—what we say is formulated in our minds—and using *mindful communication* means being aware of what's forming in our minds and making a strategic decision about whether or not to say it.

What is worrisome is the number of managers who mistakenly believe that the recipients of their criticism will learn something from it. Instead, what the recipients learn is guilt and fear of making a mistake in the future, which may lead to pretending everything is going fine with a project even when it's not, in fear of further criticism. All that they've gained is more grist for the rumination mill, and they certainly won't respect their managers. The remedy for this kind of inappropriate managerial behavior can be as simple as saying, "This could be approached in a different way, which should produce a better outcome" instead of, "You've done this completely wrong. It's just a mess." One important caveat, though, is that you can't just change the way you speak. If the attitude you're holding in your mind is that people learn from being called out, then the superficial change in speech won't fool anyone.

8. Depersonalize communication. Depersonalize communication by making a distinction between the person and her work. Comment only on the work. This all seems self-evident, but we're constantly surprised by managers who forget the principle of child-rearing—comment on the behavior, not the child—and vent their frustration and anger on their teams. When employees report in engagement surveys that communication in a company is poor, what they're most often referring to are managers who have created a blaming culture. Blaming cultures are not worth staying in.

SUMMARY

- Poor communication is one of the major contributors to disengagement and rumination among staff.

- Reframe communication based on the four steps in the Challenge of Change Resilience Training program: wake up, control attention, become detached, and let go.

- Communication has particular implications for leaders because of how it affects teams.

- Resilient leaders:

  o Communicate the four Ps of the change.

  o Talk more about what is *not* changing.

  o Identify the organization's change equation.

  o Beware of the weeds.

  o Acknowledge self-motivation.

  o Become counselors.

  o Avoid giving team members things to ruminate about.

  o Depersonalize communication.

7

CONCLUSION: PULLING IT ALL TOGETHER

The key factor that protects resilient people from stress is that they don't ruminate. Rumination is how we've defined stress in this book, and it provides the foundation for this book's unique four-step process for developing resilience: waking up, controlling attention, becoming detached, and letting go.

The new approach to stress and resilience we've described has a number of significant advantages over conventional ideas about stress management:

- It resolves the problem of misattributing stress to events, which has the inevitable consequence of making people victims of what they experience. All that events do is offer people a theme to ruminate about, which they can choose not to do.

- Using physiological rather than psychological parameters, it clarifies the arguments over whether or not stress is good for you—it clearly isn't.

- It allows a clear distinction to be drawn between so-called good and bad stress, reverting to simple language to distinguish instead between pressure and stress.

- It shows how rumination prolongs maladaptive physio-logical arousal in the absence of anything to respond to.

- It clarifies why chronic stress is harmful, but acute stress is not. Being under constant pressure is the exception rather than the norm, so what makes stress chronic is rumination, while acute stress is in fact pressure.

In addition, in our approach to developing resilience:

- We've expanded on the core program by showing how it applies to communicating more effectively, and we've added specific advice to help transform managers into resilient leaders.

- We've identified the eight personal habits that either enhance or compromise resilience, and we've outlined ways to change behavior.

- We've shown that, because the behaviors we describe are overwhelmingly conditioned habits, they can be changed with knowledge and training. The Challenge of Change Resilience Training program is an optimistic one: stress is not an inevitable part of life that has to be endured and coped with. You really can be free of it.

PRACTICING AND CASCADING THE FOUR STEPS

The first step, waking up, is challenging. The practice is to stay awake for as long as you can each time, but you have to wake up first. What can you do to maximize it when it happens? It's best to keep it as simple as possible: complex, multistage strategies are the least likely to be sustained. Most companies have a generic screen saver on work computers, but if you're able to change it, make it into this simple message: WAKE UP. Or create a poster you can pin up at your workstation, reminding you to do the same thing. For the first few weeks, you'll really notice the reminders, but be prepared for the poster eventually to become just part of the furniture. That's why the first step we established needs to be pursued as diligently as possible once you've realized how much time you might spend in waking sleep or rumination.

Once you have woken up, the second step has in fact been taken—attention is immediately available for you to control. The simplest way to establish attention control is to connect with the present, and the most direct way to do so is to connect with your senses: self-evidently, they only function in the present. It is all too easy at this point to slip back into the dreamworld, so you need to follow through with the last two steps. Another poster might be helpful. Draw a picture of someone sitting up in the loft of a barn with the flood flowing through the open doors below. Or draw a picture of a monkey that is trapped because it's holding on to the peanut. You might prefer to generate a phrase that captures the essence of the program: "Let go of the peanut," or "Shit happens. Misery is optional." (Make sure no one will be offended!) There are many such quotes scattered throughout the book, so pick one that really appeals to you.

Because these reminders will become part of the furniture, the best way to establish the practice is to do it collaboratively. Get colleagues interested in the approach. Although changing any habitual behavior takes dedication, the principles are so simple that they can be cascaded easily. Take time at a team retreat day to outline what the process is. You can then involve everyone by reminding each other to take the steps, especially if you notice that someone's attention has wandered. If you do so, make sure you have sensitivity firmly in place: if a colleague is really upset and ruminating, it might not be such a good idea at that point to tell him or her it's all just peanuts! Broach it carefully, and the collaborative approach can have a transformative effect on team culture.

In practice, most companies we work with endeavor to create a happy workforce. If you work for a large company, changing the culture of the whole organization just won't happen unless you're the CEO and have significant control over the way the organization's run. Rather than a macro approach, focus your energy where you can have an influence, which is your team.

Again, retreat days or team meetings can present ideal opportunities to introduce these ideas, and you could use our model of being above the line or below the line to illustrate them. The model was described in Chapter 3, and it has a line to represent the threshold. Adaptive, positive behavior can be placed above the line, and maladaptive, negative behavior below the line. Integrating our four steps and the eight profile measures into the model, it would look like the diagram in Figure 7.1. The listed behaviors are not exhaustive. You could limit them to just the key ones, or you could add behaviors from the program that you feel are particularly relevant for your team, and use them to develop a resilient team culture.

Adaptive Behavior	• Waking up, with attention controlled • Not ruminating about emotional upsets • Appropriately expressing how we feel, not just what we think • Not reacting in a toxic, angry manner • Dealing with things rather than avoiding and procrastinating • Finding the threshold of added value—not being a perfectionist • Maintaining a detached but compassionate perspective • Reflecting on issues rather than dreaming or panicking • Being open to change when change is needed • Focusing on solutions rather than problems
The Line	
Maladaptive Behavior	• Drifting into waking sleep • Ruminating over negative emotions • Bottling up our emotions • Acting in a demanding, toxic, and angry fashion • Putting things off to avoid dealing with them • Being a perfectionist and ignoring the 80/20 rule • Catastrophizing issues and not taking other people into account • Not being able to reflect objectively on tasks • Resisting any proposed changes in principle • Focusing on problems rather than on solutions

Figure 7.1

Presented in this way, the question of where people would prefer the team to be is a no-brainer. So many are unhappy at work. We're far more likely to be happy if we get our behavior above the line. Happiness can sound like an oversimplified generalization, and there is often a sneaking suspicion among some managers that if everyone's happy, people won't be working hard enough! There do seem to be those who aren't happy unless they have something to be miserable about, but they're the exception. The fact is that happy people work best, and although it would be difficult to say which comes first, resilient people are not only more effective and efficient but they're also happier. And why not introduce your colleagues to meditation? It would be a good idea to practice yourself first, so you can speak from experience. Meditation is far less associated with mysticism than it used to be, and we described an approach to it in Chapter 5 that is both simple and practical.

LEADING THROUGH CHANGE

We devoted part of each chapter to the implications for leaders in particular. As we've emphasized, resilience is a skill that everyone benefits from. These benefits are felt individually as well as in the social context of people's families and the organizations they work for. Personal resilience involves initiating and persisting with the practice of the four steps, but leaders are in a position of much greater influence than their team members. For example, when it comes to introducing new well-being practices such as meditation, leaders are in a much better position to do so than other employees. Leadership carries with it not just more authority but also much greater responsibility, and resilient leaders know this. Go back to our diagram: effective leaders are above the line, and they use their influence to benefit everyone.

The key message from our approach is that stress is *not* an inherent part of life.

The Challenge of Change Resilience Training program offers a new way to think about stress and resilience. The focus is on changing habitual attitudes and behavior that compromise resilience. Here's the most important message: they are just habits. They can be changed, and we have a wealth of evidence showing that change is achievable by anyone, provided that he or she is prepared to practice. What this means is that you have a choice— but the choice is obscured by habit and not being able to let go. We all know how easy it is to slip back into the old way of doing things, which is why we've shown as clearly as possible what the costs of choosing stress are: a more miserable and possibly shorter life. What's required is understanding what resilience really means, which is what we've covered in this book. Armed with this knowledge, all that's needed to acquire resilience skills and be free of the tyranny of stress is diligent practice. Nobody can become resilient for you. What better time to start than now?

APPENDIX

THE RESILIENCE
RESEARCH PROGRAM

Although Challenge of Change Resilience Training is very practical and easily understood, one of its key features is the strong research evidence on which it is based. The research forms an invisible but essential foundation, and for the interested reader, the research is described in more detail in this Appendix.

The research program commenced in the early 1980s. It was conducted primarily at the University of York in the United Kingdom and at the University of Canterbury in Christchurch, New Zealand. It all began with the simple observation that when people are exposed to disasters, afterward only a small proportion of them are diagnosed as suffering from post-traumatic stress disorder (PTSD). The reported incidence of PTSD following disasters varies from as low as 3.7 percent to over 60 percent, but most reliable studies tend very much toward the lower end of the incidence scale. The variation is attributable to a variety of factors, such as whether the disaster was natural or human-made, but it is nonetheless the case that the majority of those exposed to disasters are not subsequently diagnosed with PTSD. People's reactions tend to be distributed on a bell curve, and most fall in the middle of the distribution and are affected to some degree. At one end there is a small group who are hardly affected at all, and at the other, a small group who suffer from post-traumatic stress.

Historically, post-traumatic stress, such as the shell shock suffered by soldiers during World War I, was dismissed as a weakness. It is now recognized as a genuine disorder needing drug treatment or counseling to help people recover. A more common example would be the death of someone close to you. This is undoubtedly traumatic, and bereavement counseling is a form of post-traumatic stress counseling. As with other forms of trauma, some people require little or no counseling, while others might need years and a great deal of help to adjust. These issues aside, however, what interested us from a research perspective was why there was this difference among people after exposure to the same traumatic incident. What was it that seemed to protect some from stress but made others vulnerable to it?

Assessing personal risk factors such as this is commonly based on scores derived from psychometric scales. The process of constructing a scale is highly specialized and time-consuming, and many scales currently in use fail to meet the criteria for adequacy. Fortunately, psychometric expertise was well represented on the research team, and identifying the factors that contribute significantly to resilience was preceded by the development of psychometrically rigorous scales.

CONSTRUCTING VALID AND RELIABLE PSYCHOMETRIC SCALES

It is unfortunately true that anyone can create a scale by just thinking up statements he or she feels relate to the aspect of behavior he or she is interested in. To be useful, however, psychometric scales have to satisfy two key statistical criteria: they need to be *valid* and *reliable*. *Validity* means that the scale actually does measure what it claims to measure, and *reliability* means that it does so consistently. One form of validity is *face validity*: whether or not the statement seems at face value to be related to the behavior in question. Face validity is the basis for the informal approach we've described above, and the bias incurred is obvious. Face validity is usually formalized by consulting the literature or asking experts to provide items, but the problem is that these are still biased by the personal perceptions of the small number of people providing them.

To obtain a more objective set of items, we pioneered a technique based on a series of scenarios that were shown to people. They were asked to say how they would think, act, and feel in each of them, thus tapping into the emotional, cognitive, and behavioral dimensions. The responses were collated, and any obvious duplications were removed, but the language was not changed. A common criticism of scales is that the statements don't meet grammatical criteria, but we felt that if that's how people speak, their responses should remain in the vernacular.

The collection of statements, referred to as the *initial item pool*, was cast into questionnaire format with true or false options. These forced-choice dichotomized formats are often criticized for not offering a range of options, but if you have a scale that ranges across always, sometimes, and never as the choices, there is a drift toward the majority choosing the "sometimes" option—a drift called *regression to the mean*. Some would argue that the problem can be solved by ensuring that you have an even number of options, removing the midpoint, but the drift toward the middle of the range still occurs. We wanted people to say how they would *typically* respond to each situation, and most people are easily able to choose one or the other option to describe their typical response. Bias is further minimized by ensuring that the behavioral domain is adequately sampled and that there is a sufficient number of questions. The general rule of thumb is that at least 10 items are required.

The next step in constructing a scale is to carry out an *exploratory factor analysis* (EFA) on the responses from a large sample of people to the initial list of items. Without going into too much detail, factor analysis proceeds by intercorrelating the items in an iterative procedure aimed at grouping together items that people have responded to in a similar way. These clusters of items are called *factors*. The decision whether or not to include an item on a particular factor is based on a statistical criterion called a *loading*, which is a coefficient ranging from –1.00 to +1.00; typically, only items loading over plus or minus 0.30 or 0.40 are included on the factor. The analysis also discards items that don't load on any of the factors. The structure is then adjusted by a procedure called *rotation* to obtain the best fit for the items on each factor based on their loadings.

Factor analysis might thus be characterized as a procedure for testing *belongingness* and *redundancy*—that is, the extent to which items belong together on the different factors, as well as those that don't belong in the structure at all and can be discarded. Since each factor needs to sample the behavior domain adequately, there is an optimum number of factors represented in each collection of items, and the criterion number is indicated using a technique called a *scree test*. The factors obtained from the initial EFA are then tested by using a more advanced *confirmatory factor analysis* (CFA). This requires a separate, independent sample of participants, and if the CFA endorses the initial result obtained from the EFA, you can be confident that the factors accurately reflect the structure of the scale.

Identifying structure in this way is referred to as *factorial validation*, and the final version of the scale then needs to be tested for reliability. This includes *retest* reliability, which shows whether the scale is stable over time. The test is given to a sample of participants who complete it again after a period long enough to ensure that they can't remember how they responded the first time. Retest reliability is established if the correlation coefficient between the two administrations is sufficiently high (usually 0.80 or more). This would suggest that the scale measures stable, traitlike behavior, determined either by conditioning or by genetic predispositions. In contrast, some scales are intended to measure states, which will change depending on situations people find themselves in or maturational effects. A low retest coefficient would be expected in these cases. A further reliability test assesses whether the factors are internally consistent, which is done by calculating an index called a *coefficient alpha*. Again, alpha needs to be in the order of 0.80 and above.

Once these procedures have been completed, the scale is ready for final validation. This will involve correlating it with other scales that have been shown to measure the same construct (*concurrent validation*) and by making predictions about the expected results of experiments (*predictive validation*). For example, in the case of our rumination scale, it was predicted that high scorers would show prolonged physiological activation, which, as we'll see, proved to be the case.

This brief overview of the research process might give the impression that it unfolded in a logical and rapid sequence, but as with any scientific endeavor, many of the findings were quite serendipitous and counterintuitive. The culmination in a series of neat scales also had a long gestation period, having begun around 1980, and still continues today. Establishing the reliability and validity of a scale takes time: to develop a scale to the point where it can be used with confidence is typically at least a five-year project, and the validation of the scale continues with each new study in which it is used. All of the scales in the Challenge of Change Resilience Profile have been through this process, having been derived from longer scales that are used in the research. Only the 10 most prominent items in each scale have been incorporated into the profile, but all of the statistical evidence applies equally to them.

Even when the development phase is rigorous and lengthy, all psychometric scales are subject to bias, and they should always be interpreted with caution. The research program has ensured that the bias in the profile is minimized, but scales require honest answers. Responding to questions about one's own behavior is inevitably subjective. You might try to work out what the scale is about so that you can present yourself in the most favorable light, or an item might relate to something that actually happened to you just prior to completing the scale; your response to that item would then not necessarily be how you would *typically* behave. There are various strategies for controlling response bias, but in the training program, flexibility in the interpretation of the scores is emphasized by regarding a high score as being the range from 8 to the maximum 10, and a low score from the minimum 0 to 2.

Another feature of a well-constructed scale is that scores from a large random sample will be reflected in a bell curve, depending of course on the behavior being measured. If the behavior is very unusual, the distribution in the sample will not be bell-shaped but biased toward the absence of it, and the opposite will be true if the behavior is very common.

Responses to questionnaires are entered into a graph with two axes, one vertical and one horizontal. If you imagine that the horizontal axis represents the scores on a scale and the vertical axis the number of people getting a particular score, the scores will be distributed as a bell shape. This means that most people will have scores around the middle of the range, with fewer people as you go out to each end of the range. All of the scales in the profile approximate to a bell-curve distribution.

THE EMOTION CONTROL QUESTIONNAIRE: RUMINATION AND INHIBITION

The first questionnaire to emerge from the research was the Emotion Control Questionnaire (ECQ), subsequently expanded and revised to the ECQ2. The ECQ2 comprised four factors that we called *rehearsal, emotional inhibition, aggression control*, and *benign control*. The last two factors correlated positively with one another, and by correlating them in turn with existing questionnaires, it was clear that they formed part of the extraversion-introversion constellation of personality measures (which will be referred to from now on simply as *extraversion*). Contrary to conventional wisdom, extraversion is substantially biogenetically determined, and it forms part of a neuroscience model of individual differences called *stimulus intensity modulation*. This dimension is not implicated in making people more or less resilient, which was a helpful finding. If the key factor had a genetic component, it would be difficult to change, and there would be no point in the training!

For the *predictive validation* of the ECQ2 scale, experiments were conducted to find out how well the scale scores predict changes in behavior as a result of either experimental manipulations or natural changes. Since there is little evidence implicating extraversion in resilience, the research focused on rehearsal and emotional inhibition. The word *rehearsal* implies anticipation of a future event. The scale in the ECQ2 included preoccupation with both future and past events and experiences, so we renamed it *rumination*. Although a dictionary definition of *rumination* embraces negative and positive preoccupations, *rumination* is defined specifically in the training as "churning over the negative feelings that arise before or after an event occurs."

A number of rumination scales have been developed over the years, but the ECQ rumination scale was the first validated measure to be published. This meant that our research was starting from scratch—we had no idea how it might be implicated in resilience. In contrast, there had been a lot of research on emotional response style, and there was a general view that inhibiting emotion might be deleterious. The ECQ emotional inhibition scale had nonetheless been developed using far more rigorous techniques than was usual, including the unique process we use to derive items. For both scales, there was much research to be done to discover how they might affect resilience.

THE PHYSIOLOGY OF STRESS: THE HPA AXIS

There is probably very little in our behavior that is not influenced in some way by genetic factors, but the question is one of proportion. While there is evidence for genetic influence on personality, the effect is likely to be partial, and there are multiple genes involved. Both rumination and inhibition are predominantly learned, habitual behaviors. Like all habits, they are stable over time, but they are changeable with training and effort. An example from trauma: people who suffer from post-traumatic stress ruminate a great deal about the emotional upset after the event, but with help from counseling or drug treatments, the majority will return to their pre-trauma levels. However, even though these behaviors are learned, they are inextricably linked to the way that we respond physiologically, so instead of relying on people's subjective perceptions of how they respond, the physiological system provides an objective way of linking scale scores to stress and resilience. The research using the scales consequently focused on validation against cardiovascular and immune functions.

The biochemistry of stress is a complicated one involving a number of different physiological systems, but the focus here is on *adrenaline* and *cortisol*. Neither of these are stress hormones; they are hormones just doing exactly what they are designed to do. Arousal is preceded by a cognitive appraisal process, which in turn stimulates a neuroendocrine response involving brain tissue, primarily the hypothalamus at the base of the brain, and the adjacent pituitary gland. This complex is connected to the adrenal glands situated in the small of your back, one above each kidney. Each adrenal gland comprises an inner *medulla* and an outer *cortex*, with adrenaline secreted from the former and cortisol from the latter.

Adrenaline facilitates fighting or fleeing by increasing cardiovascular activity, reflected in increased heart rate and blood pressure to facilitate the delivery of oxygen to muscles. There is a direct neural connection between the posterior part of the hypothalamus and the adrenal medulla, so the response is extremely quick. Separately but simultaneously, the anterior part of the hypothalamus releases a hormone called *adrenocorticotropin releasing factor*, or CRF, that stimulates the pituitary gland to secrete a messenger hormone called *adrenocorticotropic hormone*, or ACTH. If the terminology seems a little daunting, it is in fact quite logical: a *tropic* effect means being drawn toward something, so ACTH is describing a hormone that is attracted to the cortex of the adrenal gland. ACTH stimulates the adrenal cortex to secrete cortisol, and since this process involves blood-borne hormones, it is consequently somewhat slower than the adrenalin response.

This is the fight-or-flight reaction we described earlier in the book, adding the freeze response that might also occur. The diagram in Figure A.1 shows the neuroendocrine pathways that are involved in provoking fight or flight via the HPA (hypothalamic-pituitary-adrenal) axis.

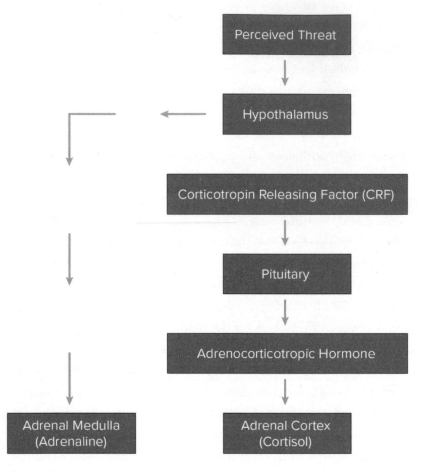

Figure A.1

Adrenaline affects primarily cardiovascular function. Cortisol has a number of effects, including acting as an anti-inflammatory so that recovery isn't impeded by unchecked inflammation. It also regulates energy, in part by accelerating glucose production and release, and it conserves energy to deal with the emergency by suspending processes that can be resumed after the emergency has passed. One of the processes that is temporarily suspended is the production of particular white blood cells. When cortisol levels are sustained experimentally, these particular white blood cell counts diminish proportionally, with a concomitant compromise of the immune response.

The initial fight-or-flight response is not stress. Rather, it is an appropriate response to demand—what we've called *pressure*. Fight or flight is adaptive in the short term, but prolonged arousal leads to sustained elevations in heart rate and blood pressure and hence cardiovascular strain, as well as impaired immune function. Stress occurs only if there is continued arousal of the HPA axis, which is what ruminating about emotional upset does. The experiments we conducted to discover the role of rumination and emotional inhibition focused on the HPA axis, assessing cardiovascular function, cortisol secretion, and immune function.

STUDIES OF CARDIOVASCULAR FUNCTION

At the initial stages of the research, the role that the new rumination scale in particular might have in the stress response was unclear, but having the psychometric scales meant that people could be selected for experiments based on their scores. Both rumination and emotional inhibition are bell-curve distributed in large random samples, so the selection of participants was from the ends of the distribution. Thus, only those who either habitually inhibited or expressed emotion and those who either habitually ruminated or not were included. The items from the two scales were nested in much longer scales that participants filled out beforehand, so they were unaware of why they had been selected.

The laboratory where the studies were conducted comprised two adjacent rooms. One was empty except for a table-and-chair workstation, while the other housed physiological monitoring equipment to measure blood pressure and heart rate. The leads from the equipment passed through a channel in the wall and ended at the workstation. When participants arrived, they were invited to sit at the workstation, and once the blood-pressure cuff or the electrodes had been placed, they were given a few minutes to get used to the situation and relax. This allowed baseline levels to be established, which for the heart rate was typically 70 to 80 beats per minute. Cardiovascular function is influenced by a range of factors such as physical fitness: regular aerobic exercise is associated with a slower resting heart rate. Lab studies are contrived to control as many of these potentially confounding variables as possible, and we factored out the effect of fitness by using step tests to estimate fitness levels.

The next step was to induce stress experimentally. Intentional stress induction poses a number of ethical challenges, and all of the strategies that we used were subject to ethical approval by the various bodies involved. The most reliable technique was to give participants a puzzle comprising a variety of small geometric shapes made of white plastic. They were given a silhouette of a target shape, and they were asked to put the pieces together to replicate the target shape. Unbeknown to them, a piece had been removed, and the task was in fact impossible. They were then told that a fictitious person in the next room was doing the same task and had finished already and that they were very slow. Finally, it was suggested to them that it was a form of IQ test. All of the participants, irrespective of their scores, showed an increase in the physiological parameters of blood pressure and heart rate—in other words, fight or flight was provoked.

The task was then stopped. Physiological monitoring continued, but the participants were asked to relax. We measured how long it took for participants to return approximately to their resting levels of the cardiovascular measures—in other words, how long it took them to recover from the arousal of fight or flight. Analyzing the results showed that those who scored high on rumination took significantly longer to recover than those with low scores, and the results from a series of studies are averaged in the representative graph in Figure A.2.

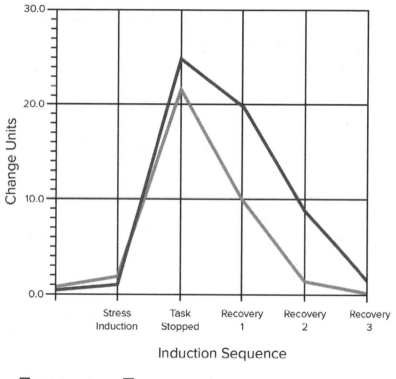

Figure A.2

Studies of speech-preparation stress by an independent research group found that high scores on emotional inhibition were also shown to delay recovery, though the effect was not as strong as the effect of rumination. However, rumination and inhibition are statistically independent. This means that any pattern of scores is possible, including scoring high on both scales, and additional experiments showed that these people took even longer to recover than those who were high only on rumination.

Research generally involves a gradual accumulation of results, but from time to time there is a eureka moment, and this was ours. We knew from other assessments during the experiments that ruminating about emotional upset made people miserable, but we now knew that it prolonged the elevated secretion of adrenaline. Rumination isn't just a symptom of stress—in the absence of rumination, there is no stress.

STUDIES OF CORTISOL SECRETION AND IMMUNE FUNCTION

The studies described above focused primarily on cardiovascular function, where the main hormonal regulator is adrenaline. The second branch of the HPA axis involves cortisol, and cortisol can be assayed from blood, urine, and saliva. Cortisol levels in both plasma and saliva samples fluctuate as the hormone is produced and then broken down by binding to protein molecules, but excess cortisol molecules that have not bound to the protein are secreted in urine (called *urinary free cortisol*). Urine samples thus provide a cumulative sample of cortisol secreted over a particular period, and urine samples were used in a naturalistic study of student nurses. They were assessed over a period during which they had to complete an important written examination. The exam results determined whether or not they were able to proceed with the course, and thus the exam represented a significant source of high pressure.

Urine samples were collected from the students immediately after the written examination. The results of the exam were made available to the groups three weeks later, and a second urine sample was then collected. The first sample thus represented the stress condition, and the second sample the control or baseline condition. Exercising control over the many variables involved is more of a challenge with naturalistic studies, but factors such as smoking behavior, coffee consumption, age, gender, and whether or not the participant had passed or failed the exam were taken into account in the subsequent analyses. The cortisol measure was based on the *proportional difference relative to the control baseline*, and the results showed that the chronic ruminators among the student nurses had a significantly exaggerated and prolonged cortisol response to the exam compared with the low ruminators.

A number of studies have implicated ruminative processes in compromising immune function. For example, the rate of healing of experimental punch-biopsy wounds was significantly slowed in samples of people who had no respite from demand, such as full-time caring for a relative suffering from dementia. These results have been confirmed in experiments where rumination was directly assessed: distinguishing between ruminator and nonruminator caregivers, the former were found to have significantly lower antibody titers against influenza inoculation than the latter group. Assessing immune function involves complex analyses that need not be described in detail here, but a study based on four different measures (leukocyte counts, lymphocyte subsets, natural killer cell activity, and proliferation of T cells) showed that ECQ rumination was a significant predictor of immune compromise, even after the effects of self-reported factors such as sadness were factored out.

The cumulative findings showed an unambiguous link between rumination in particular and a wide range of physical and psychological health measures. Low ruminators, for example, make *significantly less use of postnatal analgesics*, and the scale is significantly associated with *self-harming tendencies*. Rumination has been implicated in *prisoner behavior*, discriminating more significantly than any other measures used in the study between young offenders who had or did not have aggressive behavioral problems, with the offenders with more problems showing higher rumination scores. The scales have also been translated into several languages by colleagues working elsewhere, and the findings have been replicated across cultures.

In view of the robustness of the findings, a new questionnaire was developed focusing on the two key measures of rumination and emotional inhibition. Drawing on other projects in the overall research program the number of items in each scale was increased, and a series of factor analyses resulted in the development of a new questionnaire called the *inhibition-rumination scale* (I-RS). Experiments using the I-RS have shown that the revision of the original ECQ led to enhanced reliability and validity of the two component scales, and the Challenge of Change Resilience Profile was revised to reflect the newer sets of items.

RESILIENCE AND TOXIC ACHIEVING

A popular way of thinking about the link between stress and health came from the research on the *type A behavior pattern* (TABP). Type As are described as driven, competitive, time pressured, and often aggressive individuals whose behavior renders them more susceptible to *coronary heart disease* (CHD), while type Bs take a more relaxed approach to life and work and are less susceptible to CHD. However, closer inspection showed that the findings were equivocal, resulting in part from the construct comprising discrete components that might make differential contributions to cardiac risk. It had been suggested that there were two factors, a toxic one assessing impatience and irritability, and a benign one measuring the striving for achievement.

However, other studies found that achievement striving was a key predictor of coronary disease, along with hostility and anger. In other words, there was no clarity about the distinction between toxic and nontoxic components, and the factors that were proposed often comprised as few as four items. We conducted a psychometric study aimed at generating genuinely distinctive toxic and nontoxic factors, using the scenario technique to generate items. This resulted in a scale that distinguished between what we describe as toxic as opposed to nontoxic achieving. The components of conventional type A instruments were all correlated and couldn't be distinguished—they had conflated negative and positive elements of the drive to achieve. Studies of coronary risk are necessarily longitudinal, and the link to the new toxic component has not been assessed, but subsequent studies have shown a clear relationship between toxic achieving and prolonged cardiovascular function, as well as generally poorer health status.

Independent research on the TABP at Tilburg University in the Netherlands identified a third behavior pattern called *type D* (or *distressed*) personality, which is significantly associated with greater coronary risk. Type Ds tend to experience predominantly negative emotional responses, such as anxiety, depression, and anger, but crucially they also tend to inhibit rather than express their feelings. While there is no measure of type D in the Challenge of Change Resilience Profile, this element of type D behavior is clearly represented in scales like emotional inhibition, and independent research using the ECQ factors has shown that emotional inhibitors take significantly longer to recover from the stress induced by a speech-preparation experiment.

RESILIENCE AND COPING

We were also interested in coping, but again, the results from existing research proved equivocal, with many of the current measures claiming far too many different dimensions of coping—as many as 14 in some cases, with some factors comprising just four items. More systematic work, including factor analyses of the existing scales, suggested just three key coping dimensions, usually labeled *rational* (task oriented), *emotional*, and *avoidance* coping. Unfortunately, the items in the emotional coping factor seem to represent not coping at all, and since coping is generally thought of as facilitating resolution, avoidance also represents an absence of coping, especially in the longer term.

Going back to first principles by eliciting responses to scenarios led to the development of a new scale with an additional fourth dimension, labeled *detached coping*. In the Coping Styles Questionnaire (CSQ), detachment assesses the ability to keep things in perspective and not become overwhelmed by pressures and demands. Of the four coping dimensions, detachment is the most powerful predictor of adaptation and health, and it features prominently in the pretraining Challenge of Change Resilience Profile used in the training program. In fact, the third step in the program is to become detached.

Avoidance coping was explored further, owing to its paradoxical effects: in the short term, avoiding dealing with issues might help people to be more resilient. Not attending to an issue allows attention to be conserved and given to other demands, but avoidance does involve explicitly putting things aside. They seldom disappear, and, in the longer term, they are likely to continue to be a preoccupation. There is a modest correlation between avoidance coping and rumination, and since these preoccupations can quickly turn to ruminative thoughts about the consequences of not completing the work that's being avoided, habitual avoidance serves to compromise resilience. A further complication is that avoidance itself has at least three contributory dimensions, though reassuringly, the research has also shown that the avoidance coping scale in the Challenge of Change Resilience Profile incorporates elements of all three in a single scale.

RESILIENCE AND PERFECTIONISM

One aspect of personality that leads to unhappiness is perfectionism. Perfectionists are never satisfied with the standard of what they've done, and the paradox is that things are seldom perfect—after all, everything can be improved upon, and the nature of work in particular is that there is simply too much to do. Perfectionists habitually go on working far beyond the *threshold of added value*: the point beyond which there is little or no value added to the outcome. Perfectionism is driven by anxiety about not producing the perfect piece of work, which is why the fourth step in the training program—*letting go*—is a key strategy for perfectionists to acquire.

Further research showed that another behavior that compromises resilience, the tendency to try to control things, had a close relationship to perfectionism. What links them is anxiety—that is, concern about not delivering the perfect result for perfectionism and anxiety over the unpredictable nature of the world for habitual controllers. Just as everything can be improved upon, the simple fact is that the world is unpredictable, so the need to control it will be unremitting. Manipulating uncertainty in a lab experiment showed that participants with a greater need for control showed a significantly elevated cardiovascular response compared to those with less need for control. Findings from the research with perfectionism and desire for control were sufficiently comparable to assume that they form part of a single domain of behavior, labeled *perfect control* in the profile.

RESILIENCE AND FLEXIBILITY

The advantages of being flexible over being rigid are embedded in the folklore about oaks and reeds that we referred to in Chapter 5. Although it is just a metaphor, the implications for resilience are obvious: everything changes, and a key feature of resilience is being able to adapt to change. This can be seen as effortful and taxing if change itself is confused with stress, but in our model it will be stressful only if it provokes rumination. As we saw in Chapter 1, resilient people don't react negatively to change. Given the inevitability of change, it was hardly surprising that a measure of flexibility should emerge in the search for the characteristics of resilient people.

Perfectionists generally tend to have a rigid and inflexible way of working, but the ability to adapt to change seemed to represent a way of responding that might be independent of perfectionism. The flexibility scale was developed following the same psychometric procedures we described earlier in this Appendix, and as we anticipated, it did correlate with the perfect control measure, although the correlation was modest. What that means is that the two constructs overlap only partially, and the common feature linking them is anxiety about results short of perfection and the uncertainty of change, which is mitigated by being able to exercise control. Sadly, the control we have is always limited, so until we are able to let go, the problem will be self-perpetuating.

Adapting quickly and easily to change is preferable to disliking change and wanting things to remain the way they've always been, but being flexible can itself be a problem if you're in love with change for its own sake. In a corporate context this is especially important for managers—repeatedly moving the goalposts will only make teams feel uncertain and anxious. One aspect of the preference for change has to do with maximizing the intensity of stimulation, and this is embedded in the tendency toward extraversion. What we know is that extraversion is unrelated to rumination, and it is not implicated in resilience, but in view of the significant misunderstandings about extraversion, it is useful to provide clarification. Extraversion forms one part of a two-dimensional account of personality that includes the equally misunderstood concept of neuroticism, and it was in the process of resolving issues around neuroticism that we developed the sensitivity scale that is included in the Challenge of Change Resilience Profile.

EXTRAVERSION, NEUROTICISM, AND EMOTIONAL SENSITIVITY

Debate about how many discrete dimensions of personality there are ranges from 2 to more than 10. Many of these seemingly discrete dimensions correlate significantly with one another, indicating that they are in fact measuring slightly different facets of the same thing. In principle, science attempts to arrive at the most parsimonious explanation; in psychometric terms, that means arriving at scales that are no longer correlated. Based on factor analysis, a *first-order* extraction of scales will usually involve several inter-correlated ones, a *second-order* extraction fewer correlated ones, and so on until there are just independent scales left.

Although the issue is still hotly debated, the most recent statistical modeling has suggested that there are perhaps five discrete aspects of personality. Of these, the two that emerge most consistently are called *extraversion* (E) and *neuroticism* (N), with the former addressing the cognitive aspects of behavior, and the latter, the emotional aspects. The two dimensions are bell-curve distributed in random samples, so in practice, the majority of people would be in the middle of the distributions and have moderate levels of each. Because they are uncorrelated, it is possible to have any combination of scores, and they can be represented geometrically as four quadrants, as shown in Figure A.3.

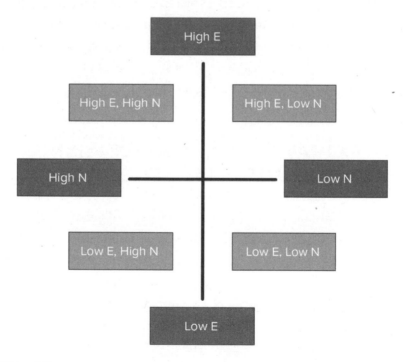

Figure A.3

There have been many attempts to account for extraversion-introversion, perhaps most prominently in the work of Carl Jung, but a more contemporary model entitled *stimulus intensity modulation* is based on physiological differences rather than just psychological ones. In this model, the extraversion dimension reflects differences in levels of *basal arousal*, which is the resting level of arousal in the brain. As with many features of the physiological system, the resting level is distributed as a bell curve, which means that most people fall in the middle of the distribution—at rest, they are at the optimal level of arousal for responding to stimuli. At each end of the distribution, there are far fewer people, with those at one end having relatively high levels of resting arousal and those at the other, relatively low levels.

The distribution of basal arousal corresponds to the distribution for extraversion, with extraverts having relatively low levels and introverts having relatively high levels. This, it is suggested, explains their behavior: typically outgoing, sociable, and sensation-seeking extraverts try to increase stimulation to maintain the optimal level, while introverts avoid stimulation in order to bring the level down to the optimum.

Anesthetics offered a way of testing the model that would not be susceptible to response bias. Administering an anesthetic would progressively suppress basal arousal until unconsciousness, so the test would be to measure levels of extraversion in patients being prepared for surgery and then determine exactly how much anesthetic was required to anesthetize them. If the model were correct, then because extraverts have lower levels of basal arousal, they should require less anesthetic to reach the *sedation threshold*. This is commonly assessed by anesthetists asking patients to count while injecting the anesthetic, waiting for slurred speech and then unconsciousness when the patient stops counting. It can be done more precisely using a measure of brain activity based on a trace from an electroencephalogram (EEG). The results of the experiment were exactly as predicted: introverts require significantly more anesthetic to reach the threshold.

An anesthetist would of course not use an extraversion test to decide how much anesthetic to use, since it is always a gradual process, rather than injecting an estimate of what's needed, but the findings have been endorsed by twin studies. Comparing one-egg (monozygous) twins, two-egg (dizygous) twins, and siblings in samples where environmental factors were controlled has indicated a substantial level of genetic determination. It is important to bear in mind that in the context of a bell-curve distribution, most people are neither particularly extraverted nor introverted (sometimes called *ambiverts*), and genetic factors are only partly what determines these individual differences. Overall, the important implication of the many studies that have confirmed this model is that this is a predisposition that doesn't change with training, but it is equally important that there is no value judgment implied by extraversion-introversion—one is not preferable to the other, and each has advantages and disadvantages. On a typical team, for example, extraverted members are likely to come up with many ideas, but without necessarily thinking through the practical implications. The introverts may not generate as many options, but they will tend to be more reflective in considering them, so harnessing these differences to strike a balance can result in highly productive teams.

There is a further important distinction that can be made within extraversion, between the two components of *sociability* (being socially outgoing) and *impulsivity* (acting without thinking). They are strongly correlated and are pooled to make up an overall extraversion score, but they can be distinguished—one of the measures we developed is for extraversion, and it allows separate calculation for each component. Impulsive extraversion can represent a significant liability, leading to high risk-taking behavior. Our work with teams indicates that extraverts should ideally show a bias toward sociability rather than impulsiveness.

One of our research concerns was the inappropriate and pejorative labeling of the emotional dimension as "neuroticism," seeming to suggest that people scoring high on a neuroticism index were neurotic. The way the construct is described implies individual differences in emotional *lability or changeability*, with those who score high on these scales being emotionally labile while low scorers are emotionally stable. We carried out a project to try to discover what so-called neuroticism might actually consist of, and what emerged was a distinction between *sensitivity to either positive or negative emotion*. The two dimensions of the new scale (the *emotional sensitivity scale*, or ESS) were characterized by negative and largely self-centered emotional sensitivity, such as often feeling sorry for oneself, and more positive and other-oriented sensitivity, characterized by being able to pick up easily on how other people feel.

Validating the scale against other existing scales included a measure of interpersonal reactivity, which provided subscales for personal distress and empathic concern. *Personal distress* indicates a personal emotional involvement in others' emotions, while *empathy* indicates concern without personal involvement. Our positive sensitivity factor correlated significantly with empathic concern but not with personal distress, and the reverse pattern occurred for the negative sensitivity factor. For the predictive validation, we focused on the positive component of the scale, selecting high- and low-scoring participants from a large sample of people who had completed the scale. Emotional tone is monitored from a variety of signals, especially facial expression, so we exposed the two groups to photographs of faces depicting a wide range of emotions. The photos were displayed very briefly (100 milliseconds), and participants were asked to identify the depicted emotion. The results confirmed what we had anticipated, with the high-scoring participants being able to accurately identify the emotion significantly better than low scorers.

Exploring the relationship between the new scale and the existing portfolio of dimensions that the research had already uncovered showed that positive sensitivity was statistically relatively independent of detached coping. Building this into a training model suggested that successful counselors, for example, would need to score high on both of these measures, what we call *detached compassion* in the resilience program. Being sensitive without sufficient detachment might easily lead to identification with the client's emotional state, while being very detached but not sensitive might mean that important emotional signals are being missed.

Unlike extraversion, which is in part determined biogenetically and hence is resistant to change, sensitivity to others' feelings is acknowledged to be changeable. Although people entering professions such as counseling are likely to self-select based on their existing predispositions, much of their training is about recognizing and enhancing emotional sensitivity. Understanding how other people feel is clearly an advantage when working with them, and not becoming overinvolved in others' emotions greatly enhances the ability to let go. Sensitivity, particularly combined with detached coping, is consequently a core feature of resilience, and it is incorporated into the Challenge of Change Resilience Profile.

Although tendencies toward introversion or extraversion can't easily be changed, they do nonetheless have practical implications. We've already mentioned the complementary roles they might play in teamwork, and they also apply to simple office arrangements like open-plan spaces. We worked with a company that had a sales team and a team of engineers on the same floor. When they shifted over to an open plan, it proved to be a disaster for the engineers, who generally tend be introverted and to prefer quiet—they just found it too noisy, while the generally extraverted salespeople thrived.

The solution was to separate the teams as much as possible and then to introduce a signaling system. A door is a signaling system: the signal is a knock, so access to you is controlled by the signal. What often happens with an open plan is that a colleague walks to your desk and says, "Sorry to interrupt, but . . ." Think back to the last time you were working on something and were interrupted like this for five minutes. When the person left, where did you start again? Not where you left off, but further back so you could remind yourself of what you were doing. That's time wasted. If there were no door, you would need a signaling system in its place. In this particular company employees had a corporate cap, the sort with the company logo on it, and that became the signal—if the cap was being worn, it was a signal not to interrupt and to come back later. There are of course limits to how much you can rearrange the office, but we've come across a surprising number of organizations that have discovered the effect serendipitously and that use various signals such as flags to communicate availability. If you have an open plan, use a signaling system if you want to avoid compromising efficiency.

FURTHER READING

The brief review of the research in this Appendix uses representative studies to illustrate the process. The list below offers a selection of published papers for the interested reader.

Birks, Y., and D. Roger (2000). Identifying components of Type-A behaviour: "Toxic" and "non-toxic" achieving. *Personality and Individual Differences, 28,* 1093–1105.

Borrill, J., P. Fox, M. Flynn, and D. Roger (2009). Students with self-harm: Coping style, rumination and alexithymia. *Counselling Psychology Quarterly, 22*(4), 361–372.

Clarbour, J., and D. Roger (2004). The construction and validation of a new scale for measuring emotional response style in adolescents. *Journal of Child Psychology and Psychiatry, 45,* 496–509.

Forbes, A., and D. Roger (1999). Stress, social support and fear of disclosure. *British Journal of Health Psychology, 4,* 165–179.

Greco, V., and D. Roger (2003). Uncertainty, stress, and health. *Personality and Individual Differences, 34,* 1057–1068.

Guarino, L. R., D. Roger, and D. T. Olason (2007). Reconstructing N: A new approach to measuring emotional sensitivity. *Current Psychology, 26*(1), 37–45.

Kaiser, J., J. W. Hinton, H. W. Krohne, R. Stewart, and R. Burton (1995). Coping dispositions and physiological recovery from a speech preparation stressor. *Personality and Individual Differences, 19,* 1–11.

Lyne, K., and D. Roger (2000). A psychometric reassessment of the COPE questionnaire. *Personality and Individual Differences, 29,* 321–335.

McDougall, C., P. Venables, and D. Roger (1991). Aggression, anger control and emotion control. *Personality and Individual Differences, 12,* 625–629.

Olason, D., and D. Roger (2001). Optimism, pessimism and "fighting spirit": A new approach to assessing expectancy and adaptation. *Personality and Individual Differences, 31,* 755–768.

Roger, D. (1995). Emotion control, coping strategies and adaptive behavior. *Stress and Emotion, 15,* 255–264.

——— (2007). Self-esteem, stress and emotion. In G. Fink (ed.), *Encyclopedia of Stress* (2nd ed.). Oxford: Academic Press.

——— (2016). Rumination, stress and emotion. In G. Fink (ed.), *Stress: Concepts, Cognition, Emotion, and Behavior.* Amsterdam: Elsevier.

———, and C. J. Hudson (1995). The role of emotion control and emotional rumination in stress management training. *International Journal of Stress Management, 2,* 119–132.

———, and J. Jamieson (1988). Individual differences in delayed heart-rate recovery following stress: The role of extraversion, neuroticism and emotional control. *Personality and Individual Differences, 9,* 721–726.

———, and B. Najarian (1989). Construction and validation of a new scale for measuring emotion control. *Personality and Individual Differences, 10,* 845–853.

———, and B. Najarian (1998). The relationship between emotional rumination and cortisol secretion under stress. *Personality and Individual Differences, 24,* 531–538.

———, and A. Raine (1984). Stimulus intensity modulation and personality: A research note. *Current Psychological Research & Reviews, 3,* 43–47.

———, G. Jarvis, and B. Najarian (1993). Detachment and coping: The construction and validation of a new scale for measuring coping strategies. *Personality and Individual Differences, 15,* 619–626.

———, G. Garcia de la Banda, H. S. Lee, and D. Olason (2001). A factor-analytic study of cross-cultural differences in emotional rumination and emotional inhibition. *Personality and Individual Differences, 31,* 227–238.

———, L. Guarino de Scremin, J. Borrill, and A. Forbes (2011). Rumination, inhibition and stress: The construction of a new scale for assessing emotional style. *Current Psychology, 30*(3), 234–244.

Stemmet, L., D. Roger, J. Kuntz, and J. Borrill (2015). General and specific avoidance: The development and concurrent validation of a new measure of avoidance coping. *European Journal of Psychological Assessment, 31*(3), 222–230.

Thomsen, D. K., M. Y. Mehlsen, M. Hokland, A. Viidik, F. Olesen, K. Avlund, K. Munk, and R. Zachariae (2004). Negative thoughts and health: Associations among rumination, immunity, and health care utilization in a young and elderly sample. *Psychosomatic Medicine, 66,* 363–371.

INDEX

A

Above-the-line
  adaptive behavior as, 165
  thinking, 71
ACTH. *See* Adrenocorticotropic hormone
Action
  adrenaline facilitated by, 14
  detachment as, 7, 86, 91
  letting go as, 7, 84, 86
Acute stress
  as not harmful, 14, 162
  as pressure, 22, 58–59
Adaptive behavior, 165
Addiction, as workplace factor, 67
Adrenal glands, 53
Adrenaline
  action facilitated by, 14
  chronic high blood pressure linked
    to, 55–56
  fight-or-flight response causing, 54, 177
  freeze reaction associated with, 55
  as hormone, 14, 177
Adrenocorticotropic hormone (ACTH),
    57–58, 177
Alcohol, 16–17
Anti-inflammatory drug, 58
Asleep
  definition of, 23
  leaders being, 39
Atherosclerosis, 56
Attachment, 91–92, 99
Attention
  communication and, 145
  control over, 7, 11, 20, 47–48, 75, 84,
    117–118, 163
  emotions fed by, 82, 84, 117
  as empowerment, 86
  as The Force, 87, 88
  intentional use of, 52
  leadership giving, 94
  in meditation, 131–133
  monitoring of, 30
  rapid attention switchers of, 26
  variations in, 48
  waking up as focusing, 47–48, 75
Avoidance
  coping and, 112, 186
  dangers of, 113
  of negative emotion, 83
  reflection compared to, 115
  as response to emotions, 114
  as rumination, 80
Awake
  being present and, 31–32, 120
  definition of, 23
Awareness
  as sensitivity, 121
  waking sleep and, 125

B

Basal arousal, 191
Behavior
  adaptive, 165
  DNA influencing, 21, 83, 103, 176
  everyday stress changing, 16–17
  happiness influenced by, 166
  maladaptive, 165
  as practice, 101
  research on, 3, 173–174
Belongingness, 172

Below-the-line
  maladaptive behavior as, 165
  thinking, 71
Blame
  managers use of, 18
  rumination reinforcing, 8
Blurred boundaries, as workplace factor, 67
Boredom, 33
Brain, measures of, 24

C

Cancer, 134
Cardiovascular function, 179–180
Case studies, controlled-trial method-
    ology use in, 3–4
Catastrophic events, 7–8
CFA. See Confirmatory factor analysis
Challenge of change
  communication and, 160
  detachment and, 118
  meditation and, 129
  profile, 21, 94, 101, 137
  research in, 169
  resilience in, 167
  training in, 2, 64, 98, 157, 162
Change
  adapting to, 126
  extraversion and, 189
  flexibility and, 125–126
  leadership in, 151, 166
  motivation to, 127
  in organizations, 154
  planning, 153–154
  purpose of, 153
  resilience, communication and, 143
Child-rearing, criticism in, 150, 160
Choice
  fight-or-flight response as, 54
  before rumination, 6–7
  stress as, 51
Chronic high blood pressure, adrena-
    line linked to, 55–56

Chronic stress
  as harmful, 14, 22, 162
  as rumination, 58, 162
Clinton, Bill, 43
Communication
  attention and, 145
  challenge of change and, 160
  depersonalization of, 147, 159
  leadership and, 153, 160
  management and, 147–148
  mindfulness in, 159
  resilience, change and, 143
  rumination influenced by, 146, 160
  skilled in, 144, 145, 151
  training in, 144
  unskilled in, 152
  waking sleep and, 145
  as workplace factor, 65, 195
Compassion
  detachment, empathy and, 122
  in detachment, 119
Confirmatory factor analysis (CFA), 172
Confusion
  over language, 4
  between stress and pressure, 5
Contagious, detachment as, 120
Control
  attention in, 7, 11, 20, 47–48, 75, 84,
    117–118, 163
  exercise in, 47
  happiness influenced by, 115–116
  research in, 188
  stress in, 12, 117
Control group
  dummy training as, 36
  seasonal effects influencing, 38
  waiting list controls as, 36
Controlled-trial methodology, in case
    studies, 3–4
Coping
  avoidance and, 112, 186
  detachment an, 76, 101, 118, 121

resilience and, 11–14, 186
sensitivity combined with, 141, 194
surviving compared to, 11
Cortex, 53, 177
Cortisol
  as anti-inflammatory drug, 58
  cortisone derived from, 58
  energy regulated by, 58
  as hormone, 177
  rumination influencing, 14, 183
Cortisone, 58
Counselors
  management as, 158
  for post-traumatic stress, 170
Creativity, 49
Criticism
  in child-rearing, 150, 160
  not constructive, 149, 158
  support compared to, 159

D
Damage, chronic stress causing, 22
Danger, of avoidance, 113
Daydreaming
  efficiency inhibited by, 20
  waking sleep comparable to, 29, 44
Death
  readjustment score of, 10
  trauma of, 10
Deep sleep
  sleep as, 24
  as unconsciousness, 27
Detachment
  as action, 7, 86, 91
  challenge of change and, 118
  compassion, empathy and, 122
  compassion in, 119
  as contagious, 120
  coping and, 76, 101, 118, 121
  as habit, 120
  as intention, 91
  leadership needing, 89

letting go and, 75–76
  as maintaining perspective, 76–77,
    82, 90, 98
  reflection requiring, 56
  seeing clearly as, 81
  sensitivity linking to, 122
Disorder, post-traumatic stress as, 80, 170
Distraction, waking sleep as, 52
Distress, as bad stress, 4
DNA, behavior influenced by, 21, 83,
    103, 176
Double blind study, 35
Dreaming sleep, 24, 27
Dreams, in waking sleep, 30
Dummy training, as control group, 36

E
ECQ. See Emotional Control Question-
    naire
EEG. See Electroencephalogram
EFA. See Exploratory factor analysis
Efficiency
  daydreaming inhibiting, 20
  waking sleep decreasing, 63, 73
Electroencephalogram (EEG), 24, 192
Emotional Control Questionnaire
    (ECQ), 61, 175–176
Emotional inhibition
  fear and, 108
  gender bias and, 107
  as habit, 108
  measuring, 105, 141
  rumination caused by, 10, 107, 128, 175
  scale for, 61
Emotions. See also Negative emotion
  attention feeding, 82, 84, 117
  avoidance as response to, 83, 114
  becoming overwhelmed by, 60
  expression of, 10, 61, 62, 74, 105–106
  flexibility restricted by, 126
  gender bias and, 62
  as human nature, 59

Emotions *(cont'd)*
memory influencing, 79
negative, 34
neuroticism and, 190
rumination upsetting, 6, 7–8, 10, 22, 23, 24, 50, 51, 134
stress and, 59
thinking compared to, 106
trauma and, 10
willingness to disclose, 105–106
Empathy
compassion, detachment and, 122
definition of, 62
leadership needing, 62, 158
problem solving using, 121
Empowerment
attention as, 86
as workplace factor, 65
Endorphins, fight-or-flight response increasing, 54
Energy, cortisol regulated by, 58
Entertainment, 3
Eustress, as good stress, 4
Everyday stress
behavior change signaling, 16–17
definition of, 16
post-traumatic stress *vs.*, 16
The evidence base, 20–21
Exercise, in control, 47
Exploratory factor analysis (EFA), 172
External disruption, 145
Extraversion
basal arousal reflected by, 191
change and, 189
impulsivity in, 192
as measure, 175
neuroticism, sensitivity and, 189
sociability in, 192

F

Factor analysis
belongingness in, 172
redundancy in, 172
relationship skills as factor in, 123
as statistical tool, 123, 172
task skills as factor in, 123
Factorial validation, 172–173
Failure, perfectionism and, 116
Fatalism, panic and, 120
Fear, emotional inhibition and, 108
Feelings. *See* Emotions
Fight-or-flight response
adrenaline caused by, 54, 177
breakdown of, 178
as choice, 54
endorphins increased by, 54
freeze reaction compared to, 28, 55
pressure, 179
provocation of, 13
as stress response, 13, 28, 53, 55, 179, 180–181
Flexibility
change and, 125–126
emotions restricting, 126
in leadership, 139
resilience, perfectionism and, 187, 188
as response, 125
The Force, 87, 88
Freeze reaction
adrenaline associated with, 55
definition of, 28
fight-or-flight response compared to, 28, 55

G

Gender bias
emotional inhibition and, 107
emotions and, 62
Glycogen, 58
Guilt, as rumination, 149

H

Habit
breaking of, 7, 176
detachment as, 120

emotional inhibition as, 108
as intention, 89
resilience as, 167
response as, 8
rumination as, 7, 68, 104, 176
strength of, 83
waking up as, 7, 31, 32
Happiness
behavior influencing, 166
control influencing, 115–116
meditation increasing, 166
well-being similar to, 133
Heart rate, 82
Homeostasis, 57
Hormone
adrenaline as, 14, 177
cortisol as, 177
HPA. *See* Hypothalamic-pituitary-
adrenal axis
Human nature, emotions as, 59
Humor, perspective as, 92, 93, 99
Hypothalamic-pituitary-adrenal axis
(HPA), 53, 178
Hypothalamus
anterior, 57
definition of, 53
posterior, 57

I

Illness, stress causing, 17
Illusion, perfectionism as, 116
Impulsivity, in extraversion, 192
Inhibition-rumination scale (I-RS), 184
Initial item pool, 171
Intention
detachment as, 91
habit as, 89
Internal disruption, 146
I-RS. *See* Inhibition-rumination scale

L

Language, confusion over, 4
Leadership

attention given by, 94
in change, 151, 166
Clinton and, 43
communication and, 153, 160
detachment in, 89
empathy necessary for, 62, 158
flexibility in, 139
liberating, 89
management compared to, 18, 148
personality and, 136
presence of mind in, 43–44
relationship skills in, 140
resilience, waking up and, 39
resilience in, 18, 39–40, 99, 137,
141–142, 160
respect for, 152
responsibility in, 166
rumination influenced by, 40, 45
SBI and, 95
training in, 4
waking up and, 39
Letting go
action of, 7, 84, 86
detachment and, 75–76
meditation and, 132
negative emotions needing, 84, 87
perfectionism and, 187
perspective and, 78
SBI facilitating, 96
sensitivity achieving, 124
Life-event scales
examples of, 9–10
interconnection between, 9–10
readjustment scores in, 9
theory and development of, 8–10
Lifespan, resilience and, 135

M

Maladaptive behavior, as below-the-
line, 165
Management
blame used by, 18
communication and, 147–148

Management *(cont'd)*
as counselors, 158
leadership compared to, 18, 148
micromanaging and, 157
psychopathy presented in, 109
toxic achieving in, 109
as workplace factor, 65
Mantra
meditation focus is, 131–132
power of, 131
as Sanskrit word, 132
Measures
of brain, 24
of emotional inhibition, 105, 141
extraversion as, 175
of personality, 102
of resilience, 102, 103, 141
tools for, 20–21, 173
of type A behavior pattern, 110
Meditation
attention in, 131–133
challenge of change and, 129
happiness increased with, 166
letting go and, 132
mantra as focus of, 131–132
mindfulness linked to, 129
process of, 130
Medulla, 53, 177
Memory, 79
Micromanaging, 156–157
Mindfulness
in communication, 159
definition of, 19
meditation linked to, 129
resilience and, 2, 19–20, 129
Misery
as optional, 11–12, 164
rumination producing, 11
stress producing, 17–18
Motivation
to change, 127
pressure as, 13

Multitasking
definition of, 26
prioritization in, 115
rapid attention switching as, 26

N
Natural killer cells (NK), 58
Negative emotion
avoidance of, 83
feeding of, 83
letting go of, 84, 87
resilience created by, 81
waking sleep combined with, 34, 45
waking up from, 34, 83
Negative thinking, 80
Neuroticism
emotions and, 190
extraversion, sensitivity and, 189
research in, 193
Nightmare, rumination as, 49, 83
NK. *See* Natural killer cells
Non Rapid Eye Movement (NREM), 24
NREM sleep, 24

O
Opportunity, waking sleep, value and, 42
Organizations
change and, 154
resilience in, 97
rumination in, 41

P
Panic
fatalism and, 120
waking sleep producing, 33
Perfectionism
failure and, 116
flexibility, resilience and, 187, 188
as illusion, 116
letting go and, 187
Performance, pressure and, 13

Personality
definition of, 102, 141
leadership and, 136
measures of, 102
Perspective
detachment as maintaining, 76–77,
82, 90, 98
humor as, 92, 93, 99
letting go and, 78
Pituitary gland, 53, 57
Planning, 72, 153–154
Post-traumatic stress
counselors for, 170
definition of, 16
diagnosis of, 169
as disorder, 80, 170
everyday stress compared to, 16
psychometric scales and, 170–171
as shell shock, 80
Practice
behavior as, 101
rumination changed with, 21
waking up requires, 63
Presence of mind
Clinton having, 44
definition of, 28
leadership having, 43–44
reflection and, 29, 47
Pressure. *See also* Chronic high blood
pressure
acute stress as, 22, 58–59
definition of, 5
fight-or-flight response and, 179
heart rate increased by, 82
as motivation, 13
performance and, 13
results of, 5–6
rumination, stress and, 6
stress from, 6, 13, 22, 69
usefulness of, 50
waking sleep, reflection and, 20
Prioritization

as continuous process, 59
managing, 60
in multitaskers, 115
Problem solving
empathy used in, 121
as reflection, 119
Psychometric scales
post-traumatic stress and, 170–171
as reliable, 171
as valid, 171
Psychopathy
management presenting, 109
in toxic achieving, 109

R
Randomized controlled trial (RCT)
control group in, 35
experimental group in, 35
results from, 37
Rapid eye movement (REM), 24
RCT. *See* Randomized controlled trial
Readjustment score
of death, 10
in life-event scales, 9
Redundancy, 172
Reflection
avoidance compared to, 115
definition of, 15, 29
detachment required for, 56
presence of mind and, 29, 47
problem solving as, 119
result of, 15
rumination compared to, 15–19, 70–
71, 85
waking sleep, pressure and, 20
Relationship skills, 123, 140
Reliability, in psychometric scales, 171
REM. *See* Rapid Eye Movement
REM sleep, 24
Research
on behavior, 3, 173–174
in challenge of change, 169

Research *(cont'd)*
  in control, 188
  Emotional Control Questionnaire
      and, 175
  factorial validation in, 172–173
  measurement tools in, 20–21, 173
  in neuroticism, 193
  peer-reviewed publications of, 3–4
  process of, 173
  RCT in, 35
  in rumination, 183, 184
  in sickness absence, 36–38
  on type A behavior pattern (TABP), 184
Resilience
  as ability, 12–13
  in challenge of change, 167
  communication, change and, 143
  coping and, 11–14, 186
  definition of, 12–13
  developing, 40–43
  flexibility, perfectionism and, 187, 188
  as habit, 167
  leadership, waking up and, 39
  in leadership, 18, 39–40, 99, 137,
      141–142, 160
  lifespan and, 135
  measures of, 102, 103, 141
  mindfulness and, 2, 19–20, 129
  negative emotion creating, 81
  in organizations, 97
  productivity improved by, 18
  rumination not in, 73
  skilled in, 68, 90, 137–138
  stress management and, 161
  toxic achievers and, 141
  training in, 136, 150
  unskilled in, 68, 91, 138
  work-life balance and, 135
Respect, 152
Response
  fight-or-flight as, 13, 28, 53, 55, 179
  flexibility as, 125

  as habit, 8
  stress as, 8, 140
Responsibility, leadership having, 166
Rumination
  as avoidance, 80
  blame reinforced by, 8
  choice before, 6–7
  as chronic stress, 58, 162
  communication influencing, 146, 160
  conundrum of, 84
  cortisol increased by, 14, 183
  definition of, 3, 8, 176
  ECQ and, 61, 175–176
  emotional inhibition related to, 10,
      107, 128, 175
  emotions and, 6, 7–8, 10, 22, 23, 24,
      50, 51, 134
  guilt as, 149
  as habit, 7, 68, 104, 176
  immune function comprised by, 17
  leadership influencing, 40, 45
  misery producing, 11
  as nightmare, 49, 83
  in organizations, 41
  planning without, 72
  practice changing, 21
  pressure, stress and, 6
  reflection compared to, 15–19,
      70–71, 85
  research in, 183, 184
  resilience not in, 73
  shifting of, 15
  stress implicated by, 6, 21, 182
  waking sleep elaborating, 34, 104

S

Sanskrit, mantra in, 132
SBI. *See* Situation, Behavior and Impact
      Feedback
Senses
  connecting with, 32, 41, 163
  waking up and, 41

Sensitivity
  as awareness, 121
  as changeable, 194
  coping combined with, 141, 194
  detachment linking to, 122
  in interactions, 164
  letting go achieved with, 124
  neuroticism, extraversion and, 189
  waking up and, 124
Shell shock, post-traumatic stress
    as, 80
Sickness absence
  primary, 35
  research about, 36–38
  secondary, 35
Situation, Behavior and Impact Feed-
    back (SBI)
  leadership and, 95
  letting go facilitated by, 96
  using, 99
Skills
  relationship, 123, 140
  requiring, 140
  task, 123
Sleep
  deep, 24
  dreaming, 24, 27
  types of, 25, 27, 146
  waking up, waking sleep and, 26
  waking up compared to, 23
Sleepwalking, 24–25, 27
Sociability, 192
Statistical tool, 123, 172
Stress. See also Distress; Eustress;
    Post-traumatic stress
  acute, 14, 22, 58–59, 162
  cancer not caused by, 134
  as choice, 51
  chronic, 14, 22, 58, 162
  controlling, 12, 117
  definition of, 7, 8 15–16
  emotion and, 59

  fight-or-flight response and, 13, 28,
    53, 55, 179, 180–181
  free of, 2, 182
  good vs. bad, 4
  illness causing, 17
  justification of, 6
  managing, 2, 15, 161
  misery produced by, 17–18
  new way of defining, 2
  not good, 5
  other people causing, 1
  pressure and, 6, 13, 22, 69
  resilience, coping and, 11–14, 186
  as response, 8, 140
  rumination implicating, 6, 21, 182
  triggers caused by, 8
  victim from, 1
Support, criticism compared to, 159
Sympathy, 122

T

T cells, 58
TABP. See Type A behavior pattern
Task skills, in factor analysis, 123
Thinking
  above-the-line, 71
  below-the-line, 71
  blanking on, 29
  feelings compared to, 106
  negatively, 80
Toxic achievers
  changing of, 111
  health risks in, 185
  individuals as, 110–111
  management as, 109
  psychopathy in, 109
  resilience and, 141
Training
  benefit of, 64
  challenge of change, 2, 64, 98, 157, 162
  in communication, 144
  face-to-face, 2–3

Training *(cont'd)*
  in leadership, 4
  in resilience, 136, 150
Trauma
  characterization of, 10
  of death, 10
  emotion and, 10
Triggers, 8
Type A behavior pattern (TABP)
  measures of, 110
  research on, 184

U

Unconsciousness, deep sleep as, 27

V

Validity
  concurrent, 173
  face, 171
  predictive, 173
  in psychometric scales, 171
  scales of, 173–174
Value
  opportunity, waking sleep and, 42
  waking sleep decreasing, 42
Victim, from stress, 1

W

Waiting-list controls, 36
Waking sleep
  awareness and, 125
  communication and, 145
  daydreaming comparable to, 29, 44
  definition of, 19, 27, 29
  as distraction, 52
  dreams in, 30
  efficiency lost by, 63, 73
  illustrations of, 29
  negative emotion combined with,
    34, 45

  not intentional, 45
  opportunity, value and, 42
  panic produced by, 33
  pressure increased by, 20
  reflection compared to, 20
  rumination elaborated by, 34, 104
  sleep, waking up and, 26
  value decreased by, 42
Waking up
  as challenge, 163
  as connecting senses, 41
  feeling of, 31
  as focusing attention, 47–48, 75
  as habit, 7, 31, 32
  leadership, resilience and, 39
  negative emotion and, 34, 83
  other people, 41
  practice required for, 63
  process of, 7, 31
  and sensitivity, 124
  sleep, waking sleep and, 26
  sleep compared to, 23
Walk-and-talk meetings, 43
Well-being
  happiness similar to, 133
  mental, 133
  physical, 133
Work Centre Ltd., 2
Work-life balance, resilience and, 135
Workload, as workplace factor, 65, 67
Workplace factor
  addiction to work as, 67
  analysis of, 66
  blurred boundaries as, 67
  communication as, 65, 195
  complexity of problems as, 67
  empowerment as, 65
  management style as, 65
Worry, 7–8

ABOUT THE AUTHORS

Derek Roger, PhD, is a U.K. Chartered Psychologist who special-izes in the physiology of stress. His work began at the University of York in the United Kingdom, where he established and directed the Stress Research Unit. He spent several years attached to the University of Canterbury in Christchurch, New Zealand, before return-ing to the United Kingdom in 2015.

The results of his original research challenged conventional ideas about stress and resilience, and they have been published in more than 100 papers, book chapters, and books. These findings led to the creation of the unique and innovative training program, Challenge of Change Resilience Training. He founded the training consultancy Work Skills Centre Ltd., which implements the Chal-lenge of Change Resilience Training program in the United King-dom and New Zealand. In the United States, the training forms part of the customized leadership programs provided by the Cen-ter for Creative Leadership (CCL).

Derek holds a bachelor's degree with joint honors in English literature and psychology, a master's degree in clinical psychology, and a doctorate in experimental psychology.

Nick Petrie is a senior faculty member at the Center for Creative Leadership. He works with CEOs and their teams to create resil-ience strategies for their organizations, particularly in periods of significant change. Nick's focus on stress and resilience began af-ter he was diagnosed with cancer in his midtwenties. After suc-cessfully applying the methods outlined in this book for himself, he spent the next 15 years teaching these tools to executives and frontline employees around the world.

Nick has worked across industries, including engineering, energy, law, banking, accounting, construction, telecommunications, and government. He has worked with clients including NASA, TD Bank, Deloitte, Red Bull, Minnesota Wild Hockey, Kellogg's, Qantas, and Comcast. Before beginning his business career, he was a professional rugby player and coach for seven years.

Nick holds a master's degree from Harvard University and bachelor's degrees in business and physical education from the University of Otago in New Zealand. He lives in Austin, Texas, with his wife and four sons.

ABOUT THE WORK SKILLS CENTRE

The Work Skills Centre Ltd. (WSC) consultancy was established in 1991 to provide a commercial vehicle for Challenge of Change Resilience Training. The training is based on Dr. Derek Roger's stress and resilience research program, which he initiated at the University of York in the United Kingdom. In 2003 Derek moved to New Zealand, where he established a WSC (NZ) branch before returning to the United Kingdom in 2015. The training forms part of customized leadership programs provided by the Center for Creative Leadership in the United States. Internationally there are currently 24 professional trainers who have been accredited by the Work Skills Centre to offer Challenge of Change Resilience Training.

For more information, visit www.challengeofchange.co.uk.

ABOUT THE CENTER FOR CREATIVE LEADERSHIP

The Center for Creative Leadership (CCL) is a top-ranked, global provider of leadership development. By leveraging the power of leadership to drive results that matter most to clients, CCL transforms individual leaders, teams, organizations, and society. Our array of cutting-edge solutions is steeped in extensive research and experience gained from working with hundreds of thousands of leaders at all levels.

Ranked among the world's top five providers of executive education by the *Financial Times* and in the top 10 by *Bloomberg BusinessWeek*, CCL has offices in Greensboro, North Carolina; Colorado Springs, Colorado; San Diego, California; Brussels, Belgium; Moscow, Russia; Addis Ababa, Ethiopia; Johannesburg, South Africa; Singapore; Gurgaon, India; and Shanghai, China.

For more information, visit www.ccl.org.